S0-BSX-678

# LSAT
## Direct

**Streamlined Review and Strategic Practice from the Leader in LSAT Prep**

## KAPLAN

PUBLISHING

New York

LSAT® is a registered trademark of the Law School Admission Council, which neither sponsors nor endorses this product.

This publication is designed to provide accurate and authoritative information in regard to the subject matter covered. It is sold with the understanding that the publisher is not engaged in rendering legal, accounting, or other professional service. If legal advice or other expert assistance is required, the services of a competent professional should be sought.

© 2009 Kaplan, Inc.

Published by Kaplan Publishing, a division of Kaplan, Inc.
1 Liberty Plaza, 24th Floor
New York, NY 10006

All rights reserved. The text of this publication, or any part thereof, may not be reproduced in any manner whatsoever without written permission from the publisher.

Printed in the United States of America

10 9 8 7 6 5 4 3 2 1

ISBN: 978-1-60714-252-2


Kaplan Publishing books are available at special quantity discounts to use for sales promotions, employee premiums, or educational purposes. Please email our Special Sales Department to order or for more information at *kaplanpublishing@kaplan.com,* or write to Kaplan Publishing, 1 Liberty Plaza, 24th Floor, New York, NY 10006.

# TABLE OF CONTENTS

## kaptest.com/publishing

The material in this book is up-to-date at the time of publication. However, the Law School Admission Council may have instituted changes in the tests or test registration process after this book was published. Be sure to read carefully the materials you receive when you register for the test.

If there are any important late-breaking developments—or changes or corrections to the Kaplan test preparation materials in this book—we will post that information online at **kaptest.com/publishing.** Check to see if any information is posted there regarding this book.

## kaplansurveys.com/books

What did you think of this book? We'd love to hear your comments and suggestions. We invite you to fill out our online survey form at **kaplansurveys.com/books.**

Your feedback is extremely helpful as we continue to develop high-quality resources to meet your needs.

# CHAPTER 1: **LSAT MASTERY**

This chapter will introduce you to the LSAT and show you how to chart a course to LSAT mastery. You'll learn about the content, timing, and scoring of the test; the different question types; and the writing sample. Strategies for getting into the right mindset to take the test, as well as checklists for complete preparation, will also be covered. Knowledge is the root of power, and by the time you have completed this chapter, you'll know all you need to begin to take control of this test.

## THE LSAT

The LSAT is designed by the Law School Admission Council (LSAC), which is the governing body of law schools. The LSAT is designed to test the critical-reading and analytical-thinking skills deemed necessary for success in the first year of law school. It is unlike any test you've taken before. Most tests are knowledge based and cover specific subject matter, whereas the LSAT is a skills-based test—there's literally no subject matter to study.

Just because it is a skills-based test does not mean you can't expect to improve your score through test preparation, however. This book was created to help you acquire the skills and strategies necessary to maximize your score on the LSAT, and this begins by getting to know the LSAT itself. On the LSAT, familiarity breeds success!

### GETTING TO KNOW THE LSAT

The same questions never appear from LSAT to LSAT. Nevertheless, the number and type of questions, the skills tested, and the directions are *always* the same. Here's how the sections break down:

| Section | Number of Questions | Time Limit |
| --- | --- | --- |
| Logical Reasoning | 24–26 | 35 minutes |
| Logical Reasoning | 24–26 | 35 minutes |
| Logic Games | 23–24 | 35 minutes |
| Reading Comprehension | 26–28 | 35 minutes |
| Experimental | 24–28 | 35 minutes |
| Writing Sample | 1 essay topic | 30 minutes |

The five multiple-choice sections on the test can appear in any order, but the writing sample invariably comes last. You will also get a 10–15 minute break between the third and fourth sections of the test.

The so-called "experimental" section will look just like one of the scored sections but will not contribute to your score; the test makers include this section to try out questions for use on future tests.

Knowing as much as you can about the test before you take it can help you take advantage of the predictable nature of the LSAT. Know the directions ahead of time so on Test Day, you can use all available time to get points. At over 3.5 hours, the LSAT is not only a test of your mind but one of physical endurance. Preparation means not just learning LSAT skills and strategies but also practicing and applying them on real tests under testlike conditions.

# QUESTION TYPES

The four scored multiple-choice sections on the LSAT that contribute to your LSAT score comprise 101 questions and just three question types: Logical Reasoning, Logic Games, and Reading Comprehension.

## LOGICAL REASONING

Each of the two scored Logical Reasoning sections contains between 24 and 26 questions, each based on a short passage (called the stimulus), which is usually in the form of an argument. Logical Reasoning questions represent about half your score!

This is because law schools want to see whether you can understand, analyze, evaluate, and manipulate arguments, a skill every law student (and practicing lawyer) must have.

On average, you should spend about 1 minute 15 seconds on a typical Logical Reasoning question.

Following is an example of a typical Logical Reasoning stimulus and question:

> A recent study has concluded that, contrary to the claims of those trying to ban cigarette advertisements altogether, cigarette ads placed on billboards and in magazines have little to no effect on the smoking habits of the smokers who view the ads. The study, which surveyed more than 20,000 smokers and solicited their reasons for continuing to smoke, found that practically no one in the survey felt that these advertisements influenced their decision to smoke.
>
> The study's conclusion is based upon which of the following assumptions?
>
> A. People do not switch cigarette brands based on their exposure to cigarette ads on billboards and in magazines.
>
> B. Cigarette ads on billboards and in magazines do not encourage nonsmokers to take up the habit.
>
> C. Banning cigarette advertisements altogether will encourage people to give up smoking.
>
> D. People are consciously aware of all the reasons they choose to smoke.
>
> E. People who decide to smoke do so for rational reasons.

## LOGIC GAMES

Your Logic Games section contains four logic games, each with between 5 and 7 questions, for a total of 23 or 24 questions. These questions test your command of detail, formal deductive abilities, understanding of how rules limit and order behavior (the very definition of law itself), and ability to cope with many pieces of data simultaneously and under strict time constraints.

On average, you should spend about eight minutes on a typical Logic Game and its accompanying questions.

Following is an example of a typical Logic Game and one of its questions:

Questions 1 to 6

During a period of six consecutive days—day 1 through day 6—a television station will broadcast six documentaries: U, V, W, X, Y, and Z. During this period, each documentary will be broadcast once, one documentary per day.

The schedule for the broadcasts must conform to the following conditions:

U is broadcast on either day 1 or day 6.
W is broadcast on an earlier day than Y is broadcast.
Y is broadcast on the day immediately before Z is broadcast.

1. Which of the following could be a list of the documentaries in the order of their scheduled broadcasts, from day 1 through day 6?

    A. U, Y, Z, W, X, V

    B. V, W, X, Y, Z, U

    C. V, X, Y, W, Z, U

    D. V, X, Y, Z, U, W

    E. X, W, V, Z, Y, U

## READING COMPREHENSION

The Reading Comprehension section consists of four Reading Comprehension passages, each about 450 words long, followed by between 5 and 8 questions, for a total of 26 to 28 questions. These long excerpts of scholarly passages are similar to the kind of prose found in law texts, and the purpose of this section is to test your ability to make sense quickly of dense, unfamiliar prose, a skill you will definitely need in law school.

You should plan to spend about eight minutes on a typical Reading Comprehension passage and its accompanying questions.

Following is an example of a typical Reading Comprehension passage and one
of its questions:

Congress has had numerous opportunities in recent years to
reconsider the arrangements under which federal forestlands are
owned and managed. New institutional structures merit development
because federal forestlands cannot be efficiently managed under the
(5)   hierarchical structure that now exists. The system is too complex to be
understood by any single authority. The establishment of each forest
as an independent public corporation would simplify the management
structure and promote greater efficiency, control, and accountability.
To illustrate how a system for independent public corporations might
(10)  work, consider the National Forest System. Each National Forest would
become an independent public corporation, operating under a federal
charter giving it legal authority to manage land. The charter would
give the corporation the right to establish its own production goals,
land uses, management practices, and financial arrangements within
(15)  the policy constraints set by the Public Corporations Board. To ensure
economic efficiency in making decisions, the Public Corporations Board
would establish a minimum average rate of return to be earned on
assets held by each corporation. Each corporation would be required to
organize a system for reporting revenues, costs, capital investments and
(20)  recovery, profits, and the other standard measures of financial health.
While the financial objective would not necessarily be to maximize
profit, there would be a requirement to earn at least a public utility
rate of return on the resources under the corporation's control. Such
an approach to federal land management would encourage greater
(25)  efficiency in the utilization of land, capital, and labor. This approach
could also promote a more stable workforce. A positive program of
advancement, more flexible job classifications, professional training,
and above all, the ability to counter outside bids with higher salaries
would enable a corporation to retain its best workers. A third advantage
(30)  to this approach is that federal land management would become less
vulnerable to the politics of special interest groups.
As a way of testing this proposal, consideration should be given to
designating a portion of the federal lands, maybe twenty-five percent,
including national forests, for management by public corporations.
(35)  The performance of the corporations would then be compared to the

performance of a comparable federal agency operation. The experiment would yield valuable information about the comparative performance of alternative institutional arrangements for managing federal lands and would provide an element of competition in federal land management
(40) that does not now exist.

1. The primary purpose of this passage is to

   A. suggest that the National Forest System is plagued by many problems.

   B. argue that it is necessary to restructure the management of federal forest lands.

   C. insist that private corporations be allowed to manage the country's natural resources.

   D. discuss the role of private corporations in the management of the National Forest System.

   E. highlight the competing needs of public agencies managing national resources.

# SCORING

You will receive a single score for the LSAT, which will fall in a range from 120 to 180. The four scored multiple-choice sections contain about 101 questions that contribute to your score (the writing sample is not scored). Here's a visual look at how these 101 questions break down by question type:

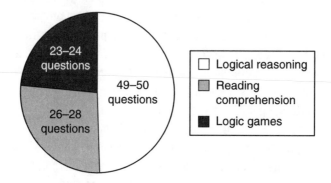

Your *raw score* is how many of these 101 questions you got correct. This raw score is then converted, using a complicated scoring formula (which changes from test to test), into a *scaled score*. The scaled score always ranges from 120 to 180. This scaled score is what is reported to the schools as your LSAT score. The scaled score always corresponds to a certain percentile, which is also given on your score report. A score of 160, for example, corresponds roughly to the 80th percentile, meaning that about 80 percent of test takers scored at or below 160.

There's no guessing penalty on the LSAT. You are not penalized for wrong answers, so you should always fill in an answer for every question, whether or not you get to it. Every question is worth exactly the same amount, so learn to recognize which questions are easy for you and answer them first; save the hard questions for if and when you get to them!

## A "Good" Score

To some extent, a "good" score on the LSAT depends on your goals and expectations and the schools to which you are applying. Nevertheless, here are a few interesting facts.

Let's say you got about half of all the scored questions right (giving you a raw score of 50). This would translate to a scaled score of 147, putting you in about the 30th percentile—not very good. However, a little improvement on the LSAT goes a long way. By getting one additional question right every 10 minutes, you'd end up with a raw score of 64, putting you in about the 60th percentile—a huge improvement! That is why it's essential for you to maximize your performance on every section.

You don't have to be perfect, however, to get a great score. On the LSAT, you can get as many as 28 questions wrong and still remain in the 80th percentile or, for that matter, get 21 wrong and still remain in the 90th percentile. It's all about doing your best on each section and knowing which questions to do and which ones to guess on if you have to.

The LSAT score is one of the most important factors in law school admissions decisions. Moreover, for most law schools, being average just won't cut it. Although the median score is around 152, you'll need a score of at least 163 to be considered competitive at most law schools. This doesn't mean that a score of 152 is bound to kill your application. Many applicants have gotten into law schools—and good ones too—with that score. However, if you're aiming high, you'll want to do better. In fact, the median LSAT scores of the most highly ranked law schools in the country (such as Yale, Stanford, and Columbia) range from the high 160s to the low 170s—in the 95th percentile and up.

# THE WRITING SAMPLE

The writing sample comes at the end of your LSAT. You're given a scenario followed by two possible courses of action, and you have 30 minutes to make a written case for the superiority of one over the other.

## WHY IS IT ON THE TEST?

The writing sample shows law schools whether you can flesh out an argument under tight time constraints and present a persuasive case for your position. Just because the writing sample is not scored does not mean that you can simply blow it off. The law schools you're applying to will receive a copy of your writing sample, and particularly if you're on the borderline of being accepted, some law school admissions officers may take a close look at your writing sample.

Following is an example of an LSAT writing sample topic:

> *The Daily Tribune,* a metropolitan newspaper, is considering two candidates for promotion to business editor. Write an argument for one candidate over the other with the following considerations in mind:
>
> - The editor must train new writers and assign stories.
> - The editor must be able to edit and rewrite stories under daily deadline pressure.
>
> Laura received a BA in English literature from a large university. She was managing editor of her college newspaper and served as a summer intern at her hometown daily newspaper. Laura started working at the *Tribune* right out of college and spent three years at the city desk covering the city economy. Eight years ago, the paper formed its business section, and Laura was named senior business and finance editor on the national business staff; she is also responsible for supervising seven writers.

Palmer attended an elite private college where he earned both a BS in business administration and an MA in journalism. After receiving his journalism degree, Palmer worked for three years on a monthly business magazine. He won a prestigious national award for a series of articles on the impact of monetary policy on multinational corporations. Palmer came to the *Tribune* three years ago to fill the newly created position of international business writer. He was the only member of the international staff for two years and wrote on an almost daily basis. He now supervises a staff of four writers. Last year, Palmer developed a bimonthly business supplement for the *Tribune* that has proved highly popular and has helped increase the paper's circulation.

Obviously there's no right or wrong answer to this writing sample topic, but there are good and bad responses. The task is to write a complete essay in 30 minutes that persuasively argues for one or the other candidate. Here's a superior response to this writing sample:

Both candidates are obviously qualified, but Laura is the better choice. For one thing, Laura has been working at the *Tribune* for eleven years and has, therefore, had plenty of opportunity to learn the workings of the paper. For another, her experience has been in national rather than international business, and national business will certainly be the focus of the *Tribune's* financial coverage. In her current capacity, she is responsible for writing and editing articles while simultaneously overseeing the work of a staff of seven. Clearly, then, Laura can work under deadline pressure and manage a staff, a capability she demonstrated at an early age as the managing director of her college newspaper. Although Laura's academic credentials may not measure up to Palmer's, her background in English, her history of steady promotions, and her work as senior national business writer—combined with a solid business knowledge and obvious drive for accomplishment—will certainly spur the department to journalistic excellence.

Palmer's résumé is admirable but is nonetheless inferior to Laura's. True, Palmer has evidently done a fine job managing the international section, but his staff numbers only four, and the scope of the venture is smaller than Laura's. True, Palmer's articles on the impact of monetary policy did win an award in the past, but since he has been working for the *Tribune*, no such honors have followed.

Not only *does* Palmer lack the English literature background that Laura has, but he also lacks her long experience at the *Tribune*. Furthermore, Palmer's editing experience seems slight, considering the length of his current tenure and the size of his staff, and while he demonstrates competence in the area of international business, he has little experience in the national business area. In light of these circumstances, the newspaper would meet its stated objectives best by promoting Laura to the position of business editor.

# TAKING CONTROL OF THE LSAT

Now that you have a general idea of what's on the LSAT and how it's scored, it's time to discuss, in a general way, how to approach the test. Subsequent chapters will fill you in on strategies specific to each question type, but to do your best on the LSAT, you need to approach the entire test with the proper spirit. That spirit is something we like to call "the LSAT Mindset."

## THE LSAT MINDSET

The LSAT Mindset is something you want to bring to every question, passage, game, and section you encounter. The LSAT Mindset means reshaping the test-taking experience so that you are in the driver's seat. It means

- answering questions **if** you want to—by guessing on the most difficult questions rather than wasting time on them.

- answering questions **when** you want to—by saving tough but doable games, passages, and questions for later, coming back to them after racking up points on the easy ones.

- answering questions **how** you want to—by using our shortcuts and strategies to get points quickly and confidently, even if those methods aren't exactly what the test makers had in mind.

The following are some overriding principles of the LSAT Mindset that will be covered in depth in the chapters to come:

- Read efficiently and critically.
- Translate what you read into your own words.

- Predict answer choices so you know what to look for.

- Save the toughest questions, passages, and games for last.

- Know the test and each of its components inside and out.

- Allow your confidence to build on itself.

- Take full-length practice tests the week before the test to break down the mystique of the real experience.

- Learn from your mistakes—it's not how much you practice, it's how much you get out of the practice.

- Look at the LSAT as a challenge, the first step in your legal career, rather than as an arbitrary obstacle to it.

The LSAT Mindset boils down to taking control, being proactive, and being on top of the test experience so that you can get as many points as you can as quickly and as easily as possible. To take control in this way, though, you have to be in command of all levels of the test.

For example, you may be great at individual Logical Reasoning questions, but that expertise won't do you much good unless you also have a plan for tackling the entire section so that you get a chance to use your expertise on as many questions possible. That's why we've developed a plan for integrating strategies and techniques on all levels of the test—from individual question strategies, to handling the mechanics of a whole section, to maintaining the right mental attitude through the entire test.

If you work hard and use this book, you will arm yourself with the LSAT Mindset come Test Day. You can use the following checklists to ensure that you will also be prepared for the test in other ways.

## LSAT CHECKLIST

### Before the Test

☐ **Get the LSAT/LSDAS Registration and Information book.**

- The registration and information book is available at most colleges and law schools and at all Kaplan Centers; you can also order it online at the Law School Data Assembly Service Website (**lsac.org**) or by phone from the LSDAS (Law School Data Assembly Service) at (215) 968-1011.

☐ **Choose a test date.**

- June is best. October is second best.

☐ **Complete and send the LSAT/LSDAS registration form.**

- Parts A, B, and D apply to the LSAT.

- Make sure to list your first- and second-choice test centers.

- Don't forget to sign the form and include payment!

- Alternatively, you can register online at the LSDAS website.

☐ **Receive your LSAT admission ticket.**

- Check it for accuracy.

- Check out your test center (you may want to travel there as a test run).

☐ **Create a test-prep calendar and make sure you're ready by the day of the test.**

- Take at least one full-length practice test in the week prior to your Test Day.

## Test Day

☐ **Make sure you have your LSAT admission ticket.**

☐ **Make sure you have one form of acceptable ID.**

☐ **Make sure you have an "LSAT Survival Kit" containing the following:**

- A watch

- A few No. 2 pencils (Pencils with slightly dull points fill in the ovals better.)

- Erasers

- A snack (There's a break and you'll probably get hungry.)

# CONCLUSION

You are now ready to start your preparation for the LSAT in earnest. The general ideas and strategies touched upon in this chapter will be explored in depth in the chapters that follow. Doing well on the LSAT involves not just understanding the question types but also knowing how to take the test in the most efficient and prepared manner. Before we move on, let's recap the LSAT test-taking strategies covered in this chapter:

- Learn how to tell tough questions, passages, and logic games from easy ones and do the easy ones first.

- Pace yourself: Most test takers won't finish every question in a set. You will pick up speed with practice but don't be afraid of not attempting to solve every problem. You can get lots of problems wrong and still get a great score.

- Guess on every question you don't get to!

# CHAPTER 2: LOGIC GAMES

This chapter details the different kinds of logic games you'll encounter on the LSAT and gives you a systematic approach to attacking them. This approach involves squeezing the most out of the information you're given before you go to the questions so you get through the game with the maximum efficiency and accuracy. We'll also discuss the best ways to manage your time strategically on this section so that on Test Day, you'll be well prepared to succeed.

## INTRODUCTION TO LOGIC GAMES

The LSAT contains one scored Logic Games section consisting of four Logic Games, each with 5 to 7 questions, for a total of 23 or 24 questions.

Unfortunately, for many test takers, Logic Games are the most intimidating and confusing question type on the test. This section also tends to be hardest one for most test takers to get through in the allotted 35 minutes.

The first time you saw an LSAT Logic Game, you probably wondered why these things were even on the test. After all, once you get into law school, you will never be asked a question like "Which teddy bear CANNOT wear the blue hat?" However, the test maker isn't really testing your ability to put blocks in order or to assign people to committees; Logic Games test three things:

1. **Your ability to use language precisely.** To do well in Logic Games, you have to understand exactly what statements do and do not mean. This kind of precision and attention to detail is important any time you encounter a complicated situation.

2. **Your ability to make deductions;** that is, to draw valid conclusions from the information given

3. **Your ability to keep track of a large number of facts**

Logic Games *do not* test your ability to draw or your ability to conceive of "the right diagram."

*Scratch work*—using your pencil to jot things down and apply the data—is a great tool. Nevertheless, it's only a tool. Your Logic Games problems will be solved not by better scratch work but by better brain work. This chapter shows you how best to organize your approach so that you can get the most out of the information that you are given before you attack the questions.

# ANATOMY OF A LOGIC GAME

Let's begin organizing our approach by breaking down a typical Logic Game and one of the questions that accompany it.

**Directions:** Each set of questions in this section is based on a set of conditions. In answering some of the questions, you may find it helpful to draw a rough diagram. Choose the most correct and complete answer to each question and blacken the corresponding oval on your answer sheet.

Questions 1 to 6

During a period of six consecutive days—day 1 through day 6—a television station will broadcast six documentaries—U, V, W, X, Y, and Z. During this period, each documentary will be broadcast once, one documentary per day.

The schedule for the broadcasts must conform to the following conditions:

U is broadcast on either day 1 or day 6.
W is broadcast on an earlier day than Y is broadcast.
Y is broadcast on the day immediately before Z is broadcast.

1. Which of the following could be a list of the documentaries in the order of their scheduled broadcasts, from day 1 through day 6?

   A. U, Y, Z, W, X, V

   B. V, W, X, Y, Z, U

   C. V, X, Y, W, Z, U

   D. V, X, Y, Z, U, W

   E. X, W, V, Z, Y, U

## BREAKING IT DOWN

Here's a breakdown of all the parts of the game and question.

### The Directions

The directions are gratifyingly straightforward—you must answer the question based on the rules you are given, and drawing a diagram is often useful. That's it.

### Number of Questions

Every LSAT Logic Games section is composed of four games, each containing between five and seven questions. Do your best on this section, you need to develop the ability to size up quickly the difficulty of a Logic Game and to decide whether to do it now or later. All other things being equal, it's better to attack a Logic Game containing seven questions than one containing five.

## The Setup

The setup gives you an overall picture of what is going on. It describes the situation, lists the entities you are dealing with, and tells you what you have to do with these entities.

If you don't understand the setup, you won't be able to answer the questions.

## The Rules

The rules provide the details about how the entities are to be selected or arranged—what entity can't be next to another, which entities must be chosen together, and so on.

It's important to realize that these rules can often be combined to form deductions that further restrict how the entities can be arranged. To do well on this section, you need to spend sufficient time getting to know the rules and drawing deductions from them before you try to answer the questions.

## The Question

The question will test how well you understood the rules and any deductions that could be made from them. Often the question will give you new information that will trigger further chains of deductions.

## The Answer Choices

You can usually eliminate at least a few answer choices if you have to guess. In a question like this, which asks you which arrangement is possible, you can eliminate those answers that are impossible by checking each answer choice against the rules.

# ATTACKING THE SETUP AND RULES SYSTEMATICALLY

The rallying cry of the Logic-Games impaired is "I could do these if only I had more time!" Unfortunately, the more one tries to speed through this section, the worse one tends to do. This is because to save time over an entire game, you must first spend time thinking through the setup and the rules. Taking a little extra time up front will enable you to recognize the game's key issues and make important deductions that will save you a great deal of time when answering the questions.

It's essential to attack the setup and rules systematically. That way you can be sure you won't miss any key elements, thus minimizing your errors. You can do this by following three steps.

## KAPLAN'S 3-STEP METHOD FOR ATTACKING THE SETUP AND RULES

**Step 1: Consider the setup.** Discover the situation, the entities involved, the action that you are required to perform, and any limitations to that action. Use this information to build a master sketch.

**Step 2: Consider the rules individually.** Either enter the rules directly into the master sketch or make a shorthand note about them next to the sketch.

**Step 3: Consider the rules together.** Look for any deductions you can find from combining the rules and enter them in the sketch.

This might sound quite complicated, but the examples that follow should make it a lot clearer.

## STEP 1: CONSIDER THE SETUP

Let's look at the following setup and see what the situation, entities, action, and limitations are.

> During a period of six consecutive days—day 1 through day 6—a television station will broadcast six documentaries—U, V, W, X, Y, and Z. During this period, each documentary will be broadcast exactly once, one documentary per day.

### The Situation

The **situation** is the game's scenario, the thing that's going on in "real life." Visualizing the real-life situation is helpful because it makes the game more concrete. Take a look at the previous setup. What are you being asked to do?

*You're being asked to design a schedule.*

## The Entities

The **entities** are the characters in the game; that is, the people or things that we need to know something about. Who or what are the entities in this game?

*The entities in this game are the six documentaries: U, V, W, X, Y, and Z.*

## Action

To understand the game's **action**, you ask: "What do I have to do with the entities?" Can you identify the action here?

*The documentaries need to be put in order.*

## Limitations

The **limitations** are the restrictions on the game's action. Can you spot any here?

Limitations: *The documentaries are scheduled one at a time, one per day.*

## Master Sketch

You can now combine these into a simple diagram, called the **master sketch**. This master sketch should be your rendition of the easiest way to visualize this game and keep track of all the entities on a piece of scratch paper. Here's a suggestion:

U  V  W  X  Y  Z

___      ___      ___      ___      ___      ___
 1        2        3        4        5        6

If a game asks you to place the entities in order, a row of dashes will help you keep them straight.

## STEP 2: CONSIDER THE RULES INDIVIDUALLY

Here are the setup, rules, and diagram again:

> During a period of six consecutive days—day 1 through day 6—a
> television station will broadcast six documentaries—U, V, W, X, Y, and Z.
> During this period, each documentary will be broadcast exactly once,
> one documentary per day.
>
> The schedule for the broadcasts must conform to the following
> conditions:
>
> > U is broadcast on either day 1 or day 6.
> > W is broadcast on an earlier day than Y is broadcast.
> > Y is broadcast on the day immediately before Z is broadcast.

U  V  W  X  Y  Z

___   ___   ___   ___   ___   ___
 1     2     3     4     5     6

We are now ready to look at the rules one at a time. A single mistake could render the entire game unsolvable; therefore, proceed with care here. You should slow down and focus on understanding what the rules mean, not just what they say.

To make the most of a rule, build the rule into the sketch directly or represent the rule with helpful abbreviations. Let's start with the first rule given.

### Rule 1:  U is broadcast on either day 1 or day 6.

Begin by building this rule directly into your sketch. We could represent it with some shorthand, such as "U = 1 or 6," but it's much easier to just build a *U* into the sketch with an arrow pointing to slot 1 and slot 6.

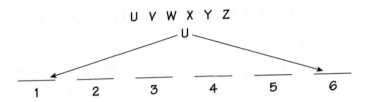

## Rule 2: W is broadcast on an earlier day than Y is broadcast.

Rule 1 gave us fixed positions for documentary U, but here we are not told much about where W and Y are placed. Therefore, we can't build rule 2 directly into the diagram. In cases like this, it's a good idea to use some shorthand notation near the diagram.

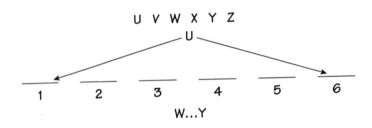

## Rule 3: Y is broadcast on the day immediately before Z is broadcast.

This rule provides even more specific information than rule 2 did. Not only is Y before Z, but Y is also immediately before Z. Here's a good way to represent this concept.

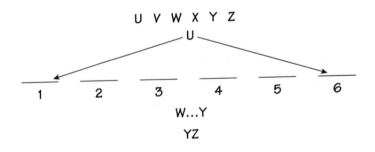

Now that we have the individual rules under control, let's move on to Step 3.

# STEP 3: COMBINE THE RULES AND MAKE DEDUCTIONS

During a period of six consecutive days—day 1 through day 6—a television station will broadcast six documentaries—U, V, W, X, Y, and Z. During this period, each documentary will be broadcast exactly once, one documentary per day.

The schedule for the broadcasts must conform to the following conditions:

U is broadcast on either day 1 or day 6.
W is broadcast on an earlier day than Y is broadcast.
Y is broadcast on the day immediately before Z is broadcast.

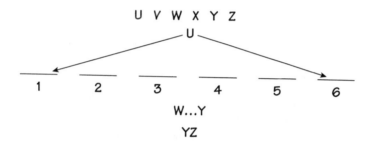

This step is vital. Questions often hinge on the deductions you can make from combining the rules. The easiest way to do this is to look for two or more rules that mention the same entity.

In this case, rules 2 and 3 both mention Y. If W comes before Y and Z comes immediately after Y, then W comes before YZ.

By combining rules 2 and 3, you can replace the two rules underneath the diagram, and replace it with your new rule

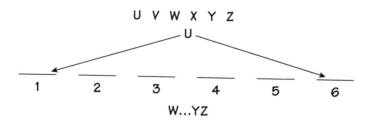

That's the major deduction you can take from this game. However, before you attack the questions, it's worthwhile spending a few seconds analyzing how the entities interact.

Think about what entities could go where. For instance, if W and Y must precede Z, then W and Y can't be in slot 6.

Now let's answer a couple of questions.

## LOGIC GAME PRACTICE

The question we've been working on is a classic example of a Logic Games question. It asks you which grouping is acceptable, so each of the wrong answer choices must violate one or more of the rules.

The easiest way to handle this type of question is to use the rules to knock off the incorrect answer choices one by one. Start with rule 1—if an answer choice does not have U in the number 1 or number 6 slot, it can be eliminated. Keep eliminating choices until you've narrowed them down to one.

During a period of six consecutive days—day 1 through day 6—a television station will broadcast six documentaries—U, V, W, X, Y, and Z. During this period, each documentary will be broadcast exactly once, one documentary per day. The schedule for the broadcasts must conform to the following conditions:

U is broadcast on either day 1 or day 6.
W is broadcast on an earlier day than Y is broadcast.
Y is broadcast on the day immediately before Z is broadcast.

1. Which of the following could be a list of the documentaries in the order of their scheduled broadcasts, from day 1 through day 6?

   A. U, Y, Z, W, X, V

   B. V, W, X, Y, Z, U

   C. V, X, Y, W, Z, U

   D. V, X, Y, Z, U, W

   E. X, W, V, Z, Y, U

Rule 1 eliminates (**D**) only, because it places U fifth. The other choices place U either first or last, so they stay in contention.

    A.  U, Y, Z, W, X, V

    B.  V, W, X, Y, Z, U

    C.  V, X, Y, W, Z, U

    ~~D.  V, X, Y, Z, U, W~~

    E.  X, W, V, Z, Y, U

Rule 2 eliminates (**A**) and (**C**), because they mix up the W–Y ordering. Therefore, now we're down to either (**B**) or (**E**).

    ~~A.  U, Y, Z, W, X, V~~

    B.  V, W, X, Y, Z, U

    ~~C.  V, X, Y, W, Z, U~~

    ~~D.  V, X, Y, Z, U, W~~

    E.  X, W, V, Z, Y, U

Rule 3 eliminates (**E**), which gets YZ backward.

    ~~A.  U, Y, Z, W, X, V~~

    B.  V, W, X, Y, Z, U

    ~~C.  V, X, Y, W, Z, U~~

    ~~D.  V, X, Y, Z, U, W~~

    ~~E.  X, W, V, Z, Y, U~~

We have eliminated (**A**), (**C**), (**D**), and (**E**). Therefore, (**B**) is the correct answer.

The following question is a little different from the last one. It starts by introducing new information in the form of an "if-then" clause. A question introduced by the word *if* contains a condition that is only applicable to that question.

---

**STRATEGY TIP**

On conditional if-then questions, you want to **build the new information into a new diagram for this question only** and then make whatever deductions you can before hitting the choices. See if you can determine how this information affects the placement of the other entities. Because these questions tend to be among the harder Logic Games questions, you may want to save if-then questions until after you've answered the other questions in the set.

---

You need to use this strategy before you look at the answer choices, so don't look at them until you've made your deductions.

During a period of six consecutive days—day 1 through day 6—a television station will broadcast six documentaries—U, V, W, X, Y, and Z. During this period, each documentary will be broadcast exactly once, one documentary per day.

The schedule for the broadcasts must conform to the following conditions:

U is broadcast on either day 1 or day 6.
W is broadcast on an earlier day than Y is broadcast.
Y is broadcast on the day immediately before Z is broadcast.

2. If the broadcast of U is scheduled for the day immediately before the broadcast of X, which of the following must be true about the schedule?

A. V or W is scheduled for day 2.

B. V or W is scheduled for day 4.

C. W or Y is scheduled for day 4.

D. Y or Z is scheduled for day 5.

E. Y or Z is scheduled for day 6.

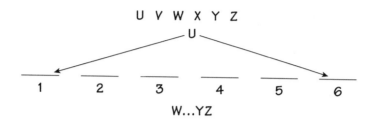

First let's start with your initial deductions. You are told X comes immediately after U, but U is in slot 1 or 6. Because X can't be after U if U is in slot 6, U and X must appear in the 1 and 2 slots, respectively. Put this in your sketch:

You can eliminate **(A)** because, according to our work, X must be on day 2.

**(B)** places V on day 4, which is possible, but also places W on day 4, which is not. Therefore we can eliminate it.

**(C)** places Y on day 4, which is possible, but also places W on day 4, which is not. Therefore we can eliminate it.

**(D)** is correct. Either Y or Z must be scheduled for day 5. If any other documentary were fifth, then there wouldn't be room for the W...YZ combination.

Eliminate **(E)** because it is possible to place Y on day 4 and Z on day 5, as we showed when we eliminated **(B)**.

The answer is **(D)**.

# SEQUENCING GAMES

Games that require you to put items in order are known as sequencing games, and they are one of the most common game types on the LSAT. You can expect to see at least one sequencing game on the LSAT you take.

Here are the setup and the rules for an example:

> At the Bedford Falls House of Reptiles, exactly six employees—F, G, H, J, K, and L—lead tours on three consecutive days—Monday through Wednesday. Each employee leads tours during exactly one shift, either the morning shift or the afternoon shift.
>
> The assignment of employees to shifts is made according to the following restrictions:
>
> > G does not lead tours during an afternoon shift.
> > F does not lead tours on the same day as L.
> > H leads tours on an earlier day than J.
> > G does not lead tours on the same day as either K or L.

## STEP 1: CONSIDER THE SETUP

Remember, your first step is to discover the situation, the entities involved, the action that you are required to perform, and any limitations to that action and then use this information to build a master sketch.

### What Is the Situation?

The situation here is the scheduling of tour guides.

### What Are the Entities?

The entities are the six employees of the reptile house, represented by the letters F, G, H, J, K, and L.

### What Is the Action?

The action is to determine the order in which the employees work.

Notice that things are a little complicated here by the fact that we have a morning and afternoon shift.

## What Are the Limitations?

The limitations are that two employees work each day, one per shift.

## Master Sketch

Here's how you might sketch this out:

| F | G | H | J | K | L |
|---|---|---|---|---|---|

|      | Mon | Tue | Wed |
|------|-----|-----|-----|
| AM   |     |     |     |
| PM   |     |     |     |

For a game that only asks you to place things in order, you just need to have a list of the entities and a sense for the slots where they will go. Here, each day has two slots—one for the morning shift and one for the afternoon shift—but we can represent that complication with rows and columns, as shown.

# STEP 2: CONSIDER THE RULES INDIVIDUALLY

## The Excluded Ends Principle

One of the most important principles in all sequencing games is the **excluded ends principle**:

- If one element precedes another, the preceding element cannot occur last, and the element that follows cannot occur first.

The excluded ends principle always comes into play in sequencing games. We used the principle informally in thinking about the previous game, but let's analyze it in a bit more detail.

If a game asks you to place the entities in order, think about where the entities cannot go. You don't have to plot out every possibility. Just think about how the entities interact. Recognize when an entity would be forced off the end of the sequence, and you'll better understand the game.

Consider this as you look at the rules one by one and build them into your diagram. Here's another look:

> At the Bedford Falls House of Reptiles, exactly six employees—F, G, H, J, K, and L—lead tours on three consecutive days—Monday through Wednesday. Each employee leads tours during exactly one shift, either the morning shift or the afternoon shift.
>
> The assignment of employees to shifts is made according to the following restrictions:
>
> > G does not lead tours during an afternoon shift.
> > F does not lead tours on the same day as L.
> > H leads tours on an earlier day than J.
> > G does not lead tours on the same day as either K or L.

## STEP 3: COMBINE THE RULES

When you have finished sketching each of the four rules, try combining any rules that mention the same entities. When you are finished, see how your final sketch compares with ours:

F   G   H   J   K   L

| | Mon | Tue | Wed |
|---|---|---|---|
| AM | | | |
| PM | | | |

G(AM)

No $\begin{smallmatrix} F \\ L \end{smallmatrix}$

H...J

$\begin{smallmatrix} G \\ F \end{smallmatrix}$ Or $\begin{smallmatrix} G \\ H \end{smallmatrix}$ Or $\begin{smallmatrix} G \\ J \end{smallmatrix}$

## SEQUENCING GAMES PRACTICE

Now let's try an exercise that will help you build important skills for dealing with sequencing games.

> At the Bedford Falls House of Reptiles, exactly six employees—F, G, H, J, K, and L—lead tours on three consecutive days—Monday through Wednesday. Each employee leads tours during exactly one shift, either the morning shift or the afternoon shift.
>
> The assignment of employees to shifts is made according to the following restrictions:
>
> > G does not lead tours during an afternoon shift.
> > F does not lead tours on the same day as L.
> > H leads tours on an earlier day than J.
> > G does not lead tours on the same day as either K or L.

What happens if a new rule is added—say, *J and K lead tours on Tuesday?*

Pencil the entities—with this new information—into your diagram so that they form an acceptable arrangement. List all the acceptable arrangements. Here's a hint: There are four acceptable arrangements.

The possible arrangements are as follows:

|     | Mon | Tues | Wed |
| --- | --- | --- | --- |
| AM  | H   | J    | G   |
| PM  | L   | K    | F   |

|     | Mon | Tues | Wed |
| --- | --- | --- | --- |
| AM  | L   | J    | G   |
| PM  | H   | K    | F   |

|     | Mon | Tues | Wed |
| --- | --- | --- | --- |
| AM  | H   | K    | G   |
| PM  | L   | J    | F   |

|     | Mon | Tues | Wed |
| --- | --- | --- | --- |
| AM  | L   | K    | G   |
| PM  | H   | J    | F   |

Now let's see how this would enable you to answer a typical question.

At the Bedford Falls House of Reptiles, exactly six employees—F, G, H, J, K, and L—lead tours on three consecutive days—Monday through Wednesday. Each employee leads tours during exactly one shift, either the morning shift or the afternoon shift.

The assignment of employees to shifts is made according to the following restrictions:

G does not lead tours during an afternoon shift.
F does not lead tours on the same day as L.
H leads tours on an earlier day than J.
G does not lead tours on the same day as either K or L.

3. If J and K lead tours on Tuesday, then which of the following must be true?

   A. F leads tours on Tuesday morning.

   B. F leads tours on Wednesday afternoon.

   C. H leads tours on Monday afternoon.

   D. J leads tours on Tuesday morning.

   E. K leads tours on Tuesday afternoon.

With J on Tuesday, H is on Monday (rule 3). Now where could G go? If G joins H on Monday, then F and L are left for Wednesday, but that's forbidden by rule 2.

|    | Mon | Tue | Wed |
|----|-----|-----|-----|
| AM | G   | J/K | F/L |
| PM | H   | J/K | F/L |

This is no good because F and L are together.

Therefore, G is on Wednesday, in the morning, according to rule 1. Who could join G on Wednesday? Only F because H and J are already placed, so F must be on Wednesday afternoon, and subsequently **(B)** is correct.

|    | Mon | Tue | Wed |
|----|-----|-----|-----|
| AM | H/L | J/K | G   |
| PM | H/L | J/K | F   |

**(A)** is impossible. **(C)**, **(D)**, and **(E)** are possible but not necessary. The answer is **(B)**.

Let's try another question where we add a new rule and see what happens.

At the Bedford Falls House of Reptiles, exactly six employees—F, G, H, J, K, and L—lead tours on three consecutive days—Monday through Wednesday. Each employee leads tours during exactly one shift, either the morning shift or the afternoon shift.

The assignment of employees to shifts is made according to the following restrictions:

> G does not lead tours during an afternoon shift.
> F does not lead tours on the same day as L.
> H leads tours on an earlier day than J.
> G does not lead tours on the same day as either K or L.

What happens if a new rule is added—say, *K leads tours on Monday afternoons, and L leads tours on Wednesday afternoons?*

| F | G | H | J | K | L | | |
|---|---|---|---|---|---|---|---|
| | | Mon | Tue | Wed | | | |
| AM | | | | | | | |
| PM | | | | | | | |

G(AM)

No $\begin{matrix} F \\ L \end{matrix}$

H...J

$\begin{matrix} G \\ F \end{matrix}$ Or $\begin{matrix} G \\ H \end{matrix}$ Or $\begin{matrix} G \\ J \end{matrix}$

Pencil the entities into the diagram with this new information so that they form an acceptable arrangement. Keep on entering acceptable arrangements until you've found them all. Hint: There are two acceptable arrangements.

Here are all the possible arrangements:

|     | Mon | Tues | Wed |
|-----|-----|------|-----|
| AM  | F   | G    | J   |
| PM  | K   | H    | L   |

|     | Mon | Tues | Wed |
|-----|-----|------|-----|
| AM  | H   | G    | J   |
| PM  | K   | F    | L   |

Now let's see how this would enable you to answer the next question.

At the Bedford Falls House of Reptiles, exactly six employees—F, G, H, J, K, and L—lead tours on three consecutive days—Monday through Wednesday. Each employee leads tours during exactly one shift, either the morning shift or the afternoon shift.

The assignment of employees to shifts is made according to the following restrictions:

G does not lead tours during an afternoon shift.
F does not lead tours on the same day as L.
H leads tours on an earlier day than J.
G does not lead tours on the same day as either K or L.

4. If K leads tours on Monday afternoon and L leads tours on Wednesday afternoons, then which of the following could be true?

A. F leads tours on Tuesday morning.

B. F leads tours on Wednesday afternoon.

C. H leads tours on Tuesday morning.

D. H leads tours on Tuesday afternoon.

E. J leads tours on Tuesday afternoon.

Because K and L are placed on Monday and Wednesday, G cannot join them (rule 4), so G is on Tuesday, the only day left. Thanks to rule 1, we also know that G is on Tuesday morning.

|  | Mon | Tue | Wed |
|---|---|---|---|
| AM |  | G |  |
| PM | K |  | L |

This eliminates **(A)** and **(C)**. We can also eliminate **(B)** because this choice directly violates rule 2. That leaves **(D)** and **(E)**. At first, it may seem as though J can work on Tuesday, but that would force H to work Monday, which in turn would force F to work on Wednesday with L.

|  | Mon | Tue | Wed |
|---|---|---|---|
| AM | H | G | F |
| PM | K | J | L |

This is no good because F is together with L.

**(E)** is impossible.

The answer is **(D)**. H could work on Tuesday afternoon, with J on Wednesday morning and F on Monday morning.

|  | Mon | Tue | Wed |
|---|---|---|---|
| AM | F | G | J |
| PM | K | H | L |

Let's try one final question where we see what happens when a new rule is added.

> At the Bedford Falls House of Reptiles, exactly six employees—F, G, H, J, K, and L—lead tours on three consecutive days—Monday through Wednesday. Each employee leads tours during exactly one shift, either the morning shift or the afternoon shift.
>
> The assignment of employees to shifts is made according to the following restrictions:
>
>> G does not lead tours during an afternoon shift.
>> F does not lead tours on the same day as L.
>> H leads tours on an earlier day than J.
>> G does not lead tours on the same day as either K or L.
>
> What happens if F leads tours on Monday morning and K leads tours on Tuesday morning?

| | | F | G | H | J | K | L |
|---|---|---|---|---|---|---|---|

| | Mon | Tue | Wed |
|---|---|---|---|
| AM | | | |
| PM | | | |

G(AM)

No F / L

H...J

G/F   Or   G/H   Or   G/J

Pencil the entities into the diagram with this new information so that they form an acceptable arrangement. Hint: There is only one acceptable arrangement.

| | Mon | Tues | Wed |
|---|---|---|---|
| AM | F | K | G |
| PM | H | L | J |

Now let's see how this would enable you to answer our final question.

> At the Bedford Falls House of Reptiles, exactly six employees—F, G, H, J, K, and L—lead tours on three consecutive days—Monday through Wednesday. Each employee leads tours during exactly one shift, either the morning shift or the afternoon shift.
>
> The assignment of employees to shifts is made according to the following restrictions:
>
>> G does not lead tours during an afternoon shift.
>> F does not lead tours on the same day as L.
>> H leads tours on an earlier day than J.
>> G does not lead tours on the same day as either K or L.
>
> 5. If F leads tours on Monday morning and K leads tours on Tuesday morning, which of the following is a pair of employees that must lead tours on the same day?
>
>   A. F and J
>   B. G and H
>   C. G and L
>   D. H and K
>   E. K and L

There was only one possible combination. With Monday morning and Tuesday morning out, the only morning available for G is Wednesday.

|    | Mon | Tue | Wed |
|----|-----|-----|-----|
| AM | F   | K   | G   |
| PM |     |     |     |

Only J can join G because F is already on Monday and putting H on Wednesday would leave no room for J. The only ones left to place are H and L, but we can't place L on Monday without violating rule 2. Therefore, L must be on Tuesday afternoon, and H must be on Tuesday morning.

|  | Mon | Tue | Wed |
|---|---|---|---|
| AM | F | K | G |
| PM | H | L | J |

The only choice that doesn't contradict this setup is (**E**). Therefore, the answer is (**E**).

# FORMAL LOGIC 101

If you never took a course in formal logic in college, that's nothing to be ashamed of. No doubt you had something better to do. You don't need a full course in formal logic to do well on LSAT Logic Games. However, the Logic Games section does test your ability to interpret Logic Games rules and make logical deductions, and this may require a quick brush-up on a few rules of formal logic.

After that, we'll look at how you can apply this knowledge to some of the tougher games that appear on the LSAT.

## IF-THEN STATEMENTS

What can—and can't—you deduce from an if-then statement? LSAT Logic Games test your ability to understand and translate if-then statements. Test takers who don't understand what they can and cannot deduce from if-then statements will definitely have trouble on this section of the test. Let's look at an if-then statement and see what we mean by this:

*If you're surfing the Internet, **then** your computer must be turned on.*

What can we deduce if you are looking at **kaptest.com**?

    A.  Your computer must be on.

    B.  Your computer must be off.

    C.  We can deduce nothing.

The original statement told us that surfing the Internet guarantees that your computer is on. Therefore, if we know that you're surfing the Internet, we know that your computer must be on. Let's try a tougher question.

What can we deduce if your computer is on?

    A.  You must be surfing the Internet.

    B.  You cannot be surfing the Internet.

    C.  We can deduce nothing.

The answer here is that we can deduce nothing from this statement. Surfing the Internet guarantees that your computer is on, but the fact that your computer is on tells us nothing about whether you are surfing the Internet. You might be surfing the Internet, but you could be doing something else with your computer, like checking your email. When you see something in the form "If X then Y" and you are told that Y is true, you don't know whether X is true. X guarantees Y, not the other way around.

What can we deduce if you are not surfing the Internet?

    A.  Your computer must be on.

    B.  Your computer must be off.

    C.  We can deduce nothing.

Nothing can be deduced from this statement. Surfing the Internet guarantees that your computer is on, but the fact that you are not surfing the Internet doesn't tell us whether your computer is on. It might be on, but it might be off. When you see something in the form "If X then Y" and you are told that X isn't true, you don't know whether Y is true.

What can we deduce if your computer is not on?

    A. You must be surfing the Internet.

    B. You cannot be surfing the Internet.

    C. We can deduce nothing.

The original statement tells you that if you are surfing the Internet, then your computer must be on. Therefore, it follows that if your computer is not on, then you cannot be surfing the Internet.

## Recap!

The following table recaps the work you've just done. What is true for this example holds for all if-then statements. Beneath each statement is its generalized form.

| If you know . . . | You can deduce . . . |
|---|---|
| **X** [You are surfing the Internet.] | **Y** [Your computer is turned on.] |
| **Y** [Your computer is turned on.] | Nothing |
| **Not X** [You are not surfing the Internet.] | Nothing |
| **Not Y** [Your computer is turned off.] | **Not Y** [You are not surfing the Internet.] |

Thus, "**If X then Y**" implies one and only one other statement: "**If not Y then not X.**"

This second statement is called the *contrapositive*. To form a contrapositive of an if-then statement, **reverse the terms and negate both terms**.

## IF-THEN STATEMENTS—FORMING CONTRAPOSITIVES

Let's see how you do at forming contrapositives. Read each of the following statements and then compare your deduction (i.e., the contrapositive) to ours.

    If Gretchen goes to the movies, then Julia goes to the movies.

This statement in shorthand: If G then J.

**Contrapositive:** If Julia doesn't go, then Gretchen doesn't go.

Shorthand: If not J, then not G.

The second statement simply reverses and negates the two terms.

Let's try one more:

> If Norbert is not in class 1, then Sykes is not in class 2.

This statement in shorthand: If N not in 1 then S not in 2.

**Contrapositive:** If Sykes is in class 2, then Norbert is in class 1.

Shorthand: If S in 2, then N in 1.

A double negative ("not not") becomes a positive.

### Recap!

Whenever you see a rule in the form of an if-then statement, form its contrapositive by reversing and negating the two terms. Remember: A double negative makes a positive.

# GROUPING GAMES OF SELECTION

Grouping games are hugely popular on the LSAT, so let's look at a classic grouping game of selection.

> A science teacher publishing a newsletter will assign exactly four topics to her students. The teacher will choose from four animal topics—ferrets, geckos, hippos, and jaguars—and four flower topics—lilies, marigolds, petunias, and roses. No other topics may be selected. The teacher will select no more than two topics concerning flowers. The teacher's assignment of topics is subject to the following restrictions:
>
>> If she assigns geckos, she must also assign marigolds.
>> If she assigns roses, she must also assign hippos.
>> If she assigns jaguars, she cannot assign marigolds.

## STEP 1: CONSIDER THE SETUP

Remember, your first step is to discover the situation, the entities involved, the action that you are required to perform, and any limitations to that action and then use this information to build a master sketch.

### What Is the Situation?

A teacher is assigning topics for a newsletter.

### What Are the Entities?

The newsletter topics are the entities. There are eight of them:

Animals: F G H J
Flowers: l m p r

Note: When the entities are divided into subgroups, your scratch work should help you keep them straight. One way to do that is to use ALL CAPS and lowercase letters.

### What Is the Action?

The action is the selecting of the topics.

### What Are the Limitations?

Exactly four topics are selected. No more than two flower topics may be selected.

### Master Sketch

Your master sketch might look like this:

```
        F G H J              l m p r
                             (max 2)

        selected  |      not selected
                  |
                  |
```

Notice that we included a note reminding us that the maximum number of flower topics is two. Other than that, we need just two columns: one for the "ins" and one for the "outs" will do just fine.

## STEP 2: CONSIDER THE RULES INDIVIDUALLY

A science teacher publishing a newsletter will assign exactly four topics to her students. The teacher will choose from four animal topics— ferrets, geckos, hippos, and jaguars—and four flower topics—lilies, marigolds, petunias, and roses. No other topics may be selected. The teacher will select no more than two topics concerning flowers.

The teacher's assignment of topics is subject to the following restrictions:

If she assigns geckos, she must also assign marigolds.
If she assigns roses, she must also assign hippos.
If she assigns jaguars, she cannot assign marigolds.

| F G H J | l m p r (max 2) |
|---|---|
| selected | not selected |
| | |

### Rule 1:  If she assigns geckos, she must also assign marigolds.
**Contrapositive of rule 1:** If she doesn't assign marigolds, then she cannot assign geckos. Here's one way to notate this information:

G → m and not m → not G

### Rule 2:  If she assigns roses, she must also assign hippos.
**Contrapositive of rule 2:** If she doesn't assign hippos, then she cannot assign roses.

r → H and not H → not r

### Rule 3: If she assigns jaguars, she cannot assign marigolds.

We could take rule 3 through the same route, but we can save time by focusing quickly on its meaning. Rule 3 means that if we have J we cannot have m and if we have m we cannot have J. In other words, we cannot have both J and m. Here's a clear way to notate this: No Jm.

Now our master sketch looks like this:

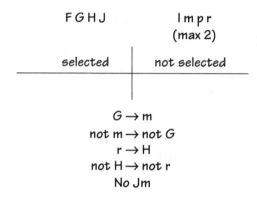

## STEP 3: COMBINE THE RULES AND MAKE DEDUCTIONS

A science teacher publishing a newsletter will assign exactly four topics to her students. The teacher will choose from four animal topics—ferrets, geckos, hippos, and jaguars—and four flower topics—lilies, marigolds, petunias, and roses. No other topics may be selected. The teacher will select no more than two topics concerning flowers.

The teacher's assignment of topics is subject to the following restrictions:

If she assigns geckos, she must also assign marigolds.
If she assigns roses, she must also assign hippos.
If she assigns jaguars, she cannot assign marigolds.

Can you combine these rules and make further deductions? Pencil into your master sketch any further deductions you can make.

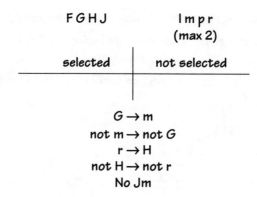

Did you combine rules 1 and 3? Because G implies m and we can't have J and m, we can conclude that any time we have G, we cannot have J. Here's the revised master sketch:

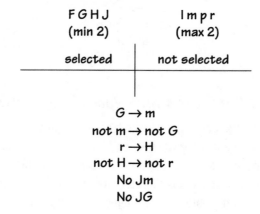

---

**STRATEGY TIP**

It is also useful to consider the numbers governing any game. In this case, four topics must be selected and no more than two of those can be flowers. Therefore, *at least two will be animals.* This is important to notate, as we've done, because whenever we can eliminate two animal topics, the other two animal topics *must* be selected.

---

Now that you've integrated your rules into your master sketch and made all the deductions you can, you're ready to attack the questions. If you haven't already done so, make sure you have a pencil and paper ready and that you've jotted down your master sketch (on the actual LSAT, you'll be doing your work in the test booklet).

## GROUPING GAMES OF SELECTION PRACTICE

Let's apply what we've learned to the following questions.

> A science teacher publishing a newsletter will assign exactly four topics to her students. The teacher will choose from four animal topics—ferrets, geckos, hippos, and jaguars—and four flower topics—lilies, marigolds, petunias, and roses. No other topics may be selected. The teacher will select no more than two topics concerning flowers.
>
> The teacher's assignment of topics is subject to the following restrictions:
>
> > If she assigns geckos, she must also assign marigolds.
> > If she assigns roses, she must also assign hippos.
> > If she assigns jaguars, she cannot assign marigolds.
>
> 6. Which one of the following is an acceptable assignment of topics?
>
>    A. ferrets, hippos, jaguars, marigolds
>
>    B. ferrets, jaguars, lilies, roses
>
>    C. ferrets, hippos, lilies, marigolds
>
>    D. geckos, hippos, lilies, roses
>
>    E. hippos, lilies, marigolds, petunias

Just as with questions that ask about acceptable arrangements, if the question asks which assignment is acceptable, apply the rules to the choices until there's only one choice left.

Rule 1 eliminates (**D**), which has geckos without marigolds.

Rule 2 eliminates (**B**), which has roses without hippos.

Rule 3 eliminates (**A**), which has the forbidden Jm.

The two-flower maximum rule that we noted on our sketch eliminates (**E**).

That leaves (**C**) as the correct answer.

> A science teacher publishing a newsletter will assign exactly four topics to her students. The teacher will choose from four animal topics—ferrets, geckos, hippos, and jaguars—and four flower topics—lilies, marigolds, petunias, and roses. No other topics may be selected. The teacher will select no more than two topics concerning flowers.
>
> The teacher's assignment of topics is subject to the following restrictions:
>
>> If she assigns geckos, she must also assign marigolds.
>> If she assigns roses, she must also assign hippos.
>> If she assigns jaguars, she cannot assign marigolds.
>
> 7. If the teacher assigns both geckos and lilies, which one of the following is impossible?
>
>    A. Ferrets are assigned.
>
>    B. Hippos are assigned.
>
>    C. Jaguars are not assigned.
>
>    D. Petunias are assigned.
>
>    E. Roses are not assigned.

Begin by placing the new information into a new sketch.

| selected | not selected |
|:---:|:---:|
| G | |
| I | |

Then we see what deductions we can make before consulting the choices. If geckos are in, then so are marigolds (rule 1). Therefore, jaguars are out (rule 3).

| selected | not selected |
|---|---|
| G | J |
| l | |
| m | |

Because we have both marigolds and lilies, we cannot have any more flowers. Therefore, both petunias and roses are out.

| selected | not selected |
|---|---|
| G | J |
| l | p |
| m | r |

The answer is **(D)**. Petunias cannot be selected.

Either ferrets or hippos could be selected, so **(A)** and **(B)** are possible. **(C)** and **(E)** must be true and are, therefore, wrong.

> A science teacher publishing a newsletter will assign exactly four topics to her students. The teacher will choose from four animal topics— ferrets, geckos, hippos, and jaguars—and four flower topics—lilies, marigolds, petunias, and roses. No other topics may be selected. The teacher will select no more than two topics concerning flowers.
>
> The teacher's assignment of topics is subject to the following restrictions:
>
> > If she assigns geckos, she must also assign marigolds.
> > If she assigns roses, she must also assign hippos.
> > If she assigns jaguars, she cannot assign marigolds.

8. If the teacher assigns jaguars but does not assign hippos, all of the following must be true EXCEPT

   A. ferrets are assigned.

   B. geckos are not assigned.

   C. lilies are assigned.

   D. marigolds are not assigned.

   E. petunias are not assigned.

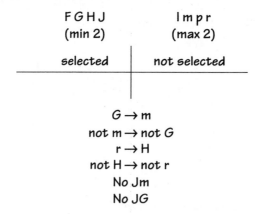

Again, we begin by placing the new information into a new sketch. The question stem tells us that Jaguars are selected but that hippos are not.

| selected | not selected |
|:---:|:---:|
| J | H |

If jaguars are in, then marigolds are out (rule 3), and so are geckos (rule 1). If hippos are out, then so are roses (rule 2).

| selected | not selected |
|:---:|:---:|
| J | H |
|  | m |
|  | G |
|  | r |

With four eliminated, everything else (ferrets, lilies, petunias) is in.

| selected | not selected |
|:---:|:---:|
| J | H |
| F | m |
| l | G |
| P | r |

From this work, you can see that every choice must be true except **(E)**, so **(E)** is the answer.

Now that you've been introduced to grouping games, let's take a look at a slightly different kind of grouping task.

# GROUPING GAMES OF DISTRIBUTION

Now let's look at a classic grouping game of distribution.

> Each of seven show dogs—S, T, V, W, X, Y, Z—is displayed in one of three cages—cage 1, cage 2, or cage 3. Cages 1 and 2 can hold three show dogs each; cage 3 can hold one show dog. No other dogs are displayed in the three cages.
>
> The following restrictions apply:
>
> > S must be displayed in cage 1.
> > T must be displayed in cage 2.
> > Neither T nor W can be displayed in the same cage as Z.
> > If V is displayed in cage 1, X must also be displayed in cage 1.

## STEP 1: CONSIDER THE SETUP

First we need to determine our situation, entities, action, and limitations, and then draw our master sketch.

### What Is the Situation?

The situation here is that the dogs are being displayed in cages.

### What Are the Entities?

The dogs are the entities. There are seven dogs: S T V W X Y Z.

### What Is the Action?

The action is distributing the dogs among the cages.

### What Are the Limitations?

The limitation is that the cages hold 3 dogs, 3 dogs, and 1 dog, respectively.

### Master Sketch

Here's what your master sketch might look like:

$$S \quad T \quad V \quad W \quad X \quad Y \quad Z$$

| Cage 1 (Max 3) | Cage 2 (Max 3) | Cage 3 (Max 1) |
| --- | --- | --- |
| | | |

A list of the entities plus three columns (one for each group) will work for visualizing. Notice that we've built in the maximum number of animals that each cage can hold; that's very important.

## STEP 2: CONSIDER THE RULES INDIVIDUALLY

Each of seven show dogs—S, T, V, W, X, Y, Z—is displayed in one of three cages—cage 1, cage 2, or cage 3. Cages 1 and 2 can hold three show dogs each; cage 3 can hold one show dog. No other dogs are displayed in the three cages.

The following restrictions apply:

S must be displayed in cage 1.
T must be displayed in cage 2.
Neither T nor W can be displayed in the same cage as Z.
If V is displayed in cage 1, X must also be displayed in cage 1.

### Rule 1 and Rule 2

S must be displayed in cage 1.

T must be displayed in cage 2.

The first two rules can be built into your sketch directly. Remember, any time you can build rules into your sketch, that is always the best option:

| Cage 1 (Max 3) | Cage 2 (Max 3) | Cage 3 (Max 1) |
|:---:|:---:|:---:|
| S | T | |

### Rule 3

Neither T nor W can be displayed in the same cage as Z.

Rule 3 is simple enough. We can't have TZ or WZ. In other words: No TZ and No WZ.

## Rule 4

If V is displayed in cage 1, X must also be displayed in cage 1.

Rule 4 is an if-then rule. Did you find the contrapositive? V in 1 forces X in 1. Therefore, if X is not in 1, then V is not in 1. This means that if X is in either 2 or 3, then V is on either 2 or 3:

V in 1 → X in 1 and X in 2 or 3 → V in 2 or 3

Now our master sketch looks like this:

S   T   V   W   X   Y   Z

| Cage 1 (Max 3) | Cage 2 (Max 3) | Cage 3 (Max 1) |
|---|---|---|
| S | T | |

No TZ
No WZ
V in 1 → X in 1
X in 2 or 3 → V in 2 or 3

## STEP 3: COMBINE THE RULES AND MAKE DEDUCTIONS

Each of seven show dogs—S, T, V, W, X, Y, Z—is displayed in one of three cages—cage 1, cage 2, or cage 3. Cages 1 and 2 can hold three show dogs each; cage 3 can hold one show dog. No other dogs are displayed in the three cages.

The following restrictions apply:

S must be displayed in cage 1.
T must be displayed in cage 2.
Neither T nor W can be displayed in the same cage as Z.
If V is displayed in cage 1, X must also be displayed in cage 1.

Can you combine these rules and make further deductions? Write down any further deductions you can make in our current sketch.

```
         S    T    V    W    X    Y    Z

       Cage 1         Cage 2         Cage 3
       (Max 3)        (Max 3)        (Max 1)
       ───────────┼──────────────┼──────────
          S       │     T        │
                  │              │
                      No TZ
                      No WZ
                  V in 1 → X in 1
               X in 2 or 3 → V in 2 or 3
```

Because we can't have T together with Z and T is in cage 2, Z must be elsewhere. Therefore, Z is in either cage 1 or cage 3.

```
         S    T    V    W    X    Y    Z

       Cage 1         Cage 2         Cage 3
       (Max 3)        (Max 3)        (Max 1)
       ───────────┼──────────────┼──────────
          S       │     T        │
                  │              │
                      No TZ
                      No WZ
                  V in 1 → X in 1
               X in 2 or 3 → V in 2 or 3
                    Z in 1 or 3
```

There are no other major deductions to make, so we're ready to move on to the questions.

## GROUPING GAMES OF DISTRIBUTION PRACTICE

Now, let's try an exercise to help build important skills for dealing with grouping games of distribution.

> Each of seven show dogs—S, T, V, W, X, Y, Z—is displayed in one of three cages—cage 1, cage 2, or cage 3. Cages 1 and 2 can hold three show dogs each; cage 3 can hold one show dog. No other dogs are displayed in the three cages.
>
> The following restrictions apply:
>
> > S must be displayed in cage 1.
> > T must be displayed in cage 2.
> > Neither T nor W can be displayed in the same cage as Z.
> > If V is displayed in cage 1, X must also be displayed in cage 1.

What happens if a new rule is added—say, *W is displayed in cage 3?*

S   T   V   W   X   Y   Z

| Cage 1 (Max 3) | Cage 2 (Max 3) | Cage 3 (Max 1) |
|---|---|---|
| S | T | W |

No TZ
No WZ
V in 1 → X in 1
X in 2 or 3 → V in 2 or 3
Z in 1 or 3

Pencil the entities into the diagram given this new information so that they form an acceptable arrangement. Hint: There are only two acceptable arrangements.

Here are all the possible arrangements:

|  | Cage 1 | Cage 2 | Cage 3 |
|---|---|---|---|
| Arrangement 1 | S X Z | T Y V | W |
| Arrangement 2 | S Y Z | T V X | W |

Now let's see how your ability to manipulate the diagram when new information is added can help you to answer a question.

Each of seven show dogs—S, T, V, W, X, Y, Z—is displayed in one of three cages—cage 1, cage 2, or cage 3. Cages 1 and 2 can hold three show dogs each; cage 3 can hold one show dog. No other dogs are displayed in the three cages.

The following restrictions apply:

S must be displayed in cage 1.
T must be displayed in cage 2.
Neither T nor W can be displayed in the same cage as Z.
If V is displayed in cage 1, X must also be displayed in cage 1.

9. If W is displayed in cage 3, which one of the following dogs must be displayed in cage 2?

   A. S

   B. V

   C. X

   D. Y

   E. Z

With W in cage 3, cage 3 is full, and the only place for Z is cage 1.

| Cage 1 (Max 3) | Cage 2 (Max 3) | Cage 3 (Max 1) |
|---|---|---|
| S Z | T | W |

Now here's the tough part: we don't have room for both V and X in cage 1, so we can't place V in cage 1. If we did, we'd need to put X in cage 1 as well, and we don't have the room because cage 1 will only hold three dogs, not four.

| Cage 1 (Max 3) | Cage 2 (Max 3) | Cage 3 (Max 1) |
|---|---|---|
| S Z | T V | W |

(A) and (E) are impossible. (C) and (D) could be true but do not have to be true. Remember, the question asked for what *must* be true.

The answer is (B).

Let's apply another hypothetical rule to our diagram and see what happens.

> Each of seven show dogs—S, T, V, W, X, Y, Z—is displayed in one of three cages—cage 1, cage 2, or cage 3. Cages 1 and 2 can hold three show dogs each; cage 3 can hold one show dog. No other dogs are displayed in the three cages.
>
> The following restrictions apply:
>
> > S must be displayed in cage 1.
> > T must be displayed in cage 2.
> > Neither T nor W can be displayed in the same cage as Z.
> > If V is displayed in cage 1, X must also be displayed in cage 1.

What happens if X is displayed in cage 3?

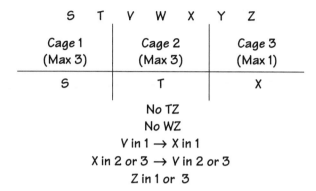

Pencil the entities into the diagram given this new information so that they form an acceptable arrangement. Hint: There is only one acceptable arrangement.

Here is the acceptable arrangement:

|  | Cage 1 | Cage 2 | Cage 3 |
|---|---|---|---|
| Arrangement 1 | S Y Z | T W V | X |

Now try attacking this question.

> Each of seven show dogs—S, T, V, W, X, Y, Z—is displayed in one of three cages—cage 1, cage 2, or cage 3. Cages 1 and 2 can hold three show dogs each; cage 3 can hold one show dog. No other dogs are displayed in the three cages.
>
> The following restrictions apply:
>
> S must be displayed in cage 1.
> T must be displayed in cage 2.
> Neither T nor W can be displayed in the same cage as Z.
> If V is displayed in cage 1, X must also be displayed in cage 1.

10. If X is displayed in cage 3, how many different assignments of dogs to cages are possible?

    A. 1

    B. 2

    C. 3

    D. 4

    E. 5

X in cage 3 means we can't have V in cage 1 (contrapositive of rule 4). Furthermore, because cage 3 is full, V has to go in cage 2.

| Cage 1 (Max 3) | Cage 2 (Max 3) | Cage 3 (Max 1) |
| --- | --- | --- |
| S | T V | X |

Z now has nowhere to go but cage 1, which means that W must go in cage 2 (rule 3).

| Cage 1 (Max 3) | Cage 2 (Max 3) | Cage 3 (Max 1) |
| --- | --- | --- |
| S Z | T V W | X |

Y is the only dog left, so Y goes in cage 1, the only cage with a space left.

| Cage 1 (Max 3) | Cage 2 (Max 3) | Cage 3 (Max 1) |
| --- | --- | --- |
| S Y Z | T V W | X |

There's just one combination. Therefore, **(A)** is correct.

Let's apply one last hypothetical to our diagram and see what happens.

> Each of seven show dogs—S, T, V, W, X, Y, Z—is displayed in one of
> three cages—cage 1, cage 2, or cage 3. Cages 1 and 2 can hold three
> show dogs each; cage 3 can hold one show dog. No other dogs are
> displayed in the three cages.
>
> The following restrictions apply:
>
> > S must be displayed in cage 1.
> > T must be displayed in cage 2.
> > Neither T nor W can be displayed in the same cage as Z.
> > If V is displayed in cage 1, X must also be displayed in cage 1.

What happens if W and X are displayed together?

| S | T | V | W | X | Y | Z |
|---|---|---|---|---|---|---|

| Cage 1 (Max 3) | Cage 2 (Max 3) | Cage 3 (Max 1) |
|---|---|---|
| S | T | |

No TZ
No WZ
V in 1 → X in 1
X in 2 or 3 → V in 2 or 3
Z in 1 or 3
W → X
X → W

Pencil the entities into the diagram given this new information so that they form an
acceptable arrangement. Hint: There are two acceptable arrangements.

Here are all the possible arrangements:

|  | Cage 1 | Cage 2 | Cage 3 |
| --- | --- | --- | --- |
| Arrangement 1 | S W X | T Y V | Z |
| Arrangement 2 | S Y Z | T W X | V |

Now try one last question.

Each of seven show dogs—S, T, V, W, X, Y, Z—is displayed in one of three cages—cage 1, cage 2, or cage 3. Cages 1 and 2 can hold three show dogs each; cage 3 can hold one show dog. No other dogs are displayed in the three cages.

The following restrictions apply:

S must be displayed in cage 1.
T must be displayed in cage 2.
Neither T nor W can be displayed in the same cage as Z.
If V is displayed in cage 1, X must also be displayed in cage 1.

11. If W and X are displayed together, which of the following is a complete and accurate list of the dogs that could be displayed in cage 3?

   A. V

   B. Z

   C. V, Y

   D. V, Z

   E. V, Y, Z

Sometimes there's nothing to do but work out the combinations. If W and X are together, where could they go? If they're both in cage 1, then Z must go in cage 3, as per the combination of rules 2 and 3. Therefore, V and Y are left to go in cage 2.

| Cage 1 (Max 3) | Cage 2 (Max 3) | Cage 3 (Max 1) |
|---|---|---|
| S W X | T Y V | Z |

That's one possible arrangement, so any choice that omits Z must be wrong. Therefore, **(A)** and **(C)** are wrong. The only other place for W and X is cage 2. If X is in cage 2, then V cannot be in cage 1 (contrapositive of rule 4), so V is in cage 3, leaving Y and Z in cage 1.

| Cage 1 (Max 3) | Cage 2 (Max 3) | Cage 3 (Max 1) |
|---|---|---|
| S Y Z | T W X | V |

This combination is acceptable as well, so we know that V is part of our answer. That eliminates **(B)**. Now, we're down to **(D)** and **(E)**, and the only difference is that **(E)** contains Y—and that isn't possible because we've already worked out the only possibilities. If W and X are in cage 1, then Z is in cage 3. If W and X are in cage 2, then V is in cage 3. That's enough to pick **(D)**. You could have spent more time disproving **(E)**, but that isn't necessary.

The answer is **(D)**.

# OTHER TYPES OF LSAT LOGIC GAMES

We've now examined sequencing games, grouping games of selection, and grouping games of distribution. These are three of most common types of Logic Games that appear on the LSAT, and you're bound to see several of them on the LSAT you take.

Let's take a quick look at two other common types of Logic Game: matching games and hybrid games.

## MATCHING GAMES

Here's an example of a typical matching game question:

> Each of the homes of four families—the Crosbys, the Donovans, the Roses, and the Steins—suffered at least one out of a total of nine instances of damage as a result of a storm. Three homes suffered broken windows, two suffered flooding, two suffered power outages, one suffered cracked gutters, and one suffered roof damage.
>
> > The Crosbys' home and the Roses' home suffered no damages in common.
> > The Donovans' home suffered more instances of damage than did the Steins' home.
> > The Steins' home suffered roof damage.

Some things to note about matching games are as follows:

- Matching games are so called because your task is to match different qualities, in this case instances of house damage, to different elements, in this case family homes.

- In visualizing matching games, it's often helpful to use grids or lists for your master sketch. As noted before, however, there's no one correct way to diagram a game, and it's important to be flexible and remember: thinking must always precede sketching.

- These games may include if-then rules, which can be handled by applying the contrapositives.

- You can usually make several important deductions by combining the rules on this game type.

- These are often the most complicated games found on the LSAT, so you're probably best off doing these games last.

## HYBRID GAMES

Following is a typical example of a hybrid game:

> In each of the first three months of a sales cycle, a furniture retailer will place items on sale. The only items that can be placed on sale are nightstands, ottomans, paintings, rugs, sofas, and tables. Each item will be placed on sale exactly once, and each item placed on sale remains on sale for an entire month.
>
> The retailer's selections of sales items must meet the following conditions:
>
> > No other items are on sale during the month in which sofas are on sale.
> > Tables are on sale during an earlier month than nightstands.
> > Ottomans and paintings cannot be on sale during the same month.

Some things to note about hybrid games are as follows:

- Hybrid games are so called because they incorporate elements of two (or possibly more) other types of games. For instance, this game is essentially a grouping game, but it requires you place the entities in order from first to third month, so it contains features of a sequencing game. Therefore it's a grouping/sequencing hybrid game. You could also see a sequencing/matching, grouping/matching, or even possibly a sequencing/grouping/matching hybrid game on your LSAT.

- Not every difficult game is hybrid, and not every hybrid game is difficult. Hybrid games have the potential to be more difficult than other types of games, but they're not all that alien. If you can handle sequencing games and grouping games, you can handle hybrid games that contain elements of both.

- Start with the action that's easier to identify and then add the other. For instance, here we essentially have a grouping game, except that the groups themselves (that is, the months) are in order.

> **STRATEGY TIP**
> Always work on questions systematically. Just as easy games have hard questions, even the hardest games have easy questions. If nothing else, you should always answer "acceptability" questions.

Remember, familiarity breeds success on the LSAT! If you have the time, spend it with our additional practice materials getting to know all the question types that can appear on the LSAT. Kaplan's *LSAT Logic Game Workbook* is a great resource for even more practice.

# CONCLUSION

Here are the strategies to keep in mind as you work your way through the LSAT Logic Games section.

## LOGIC GAMES SECTION MANAGEMENT

### Preview the Section
By this, we mean you should literally flip through the pages, having a glance at each game and deciding which games look the easiest and most familiar to you. Previewing, of course, is not foolproof. Some easy-looking games can turn out to be killers, but it works much more often than not.

### Do the Easiest Games First
This way you'll build up your pace and confidence as you go along, so you'll be better prepared to handle the tough games when and if you get to them. If you achieve nothing more than saving the hardest game for last, this strategy is well worth the effort.

### Don't Be Scared Off by Games with Lots of Rules
Sometimes lots of rules can work to your advantage. The more rules you're given, the more definite and concrete the game situation is, and the easier it will be to answer the questions. Games with few rules often turn out to be tough, because they're inherently ambiguous.

## Pace Yourself

Remember, you have slightly more than eight minutes on average to handle each game and its associated questions. If you spend less time on an earlier, easier game, that's great; you'll have that much more time to handle a tougher game. Don't obsess on the clock, but don't let your time be swallowed up by a single hard game or, even worse, a single hard question.

## Don't Be Afraid to Give Up and Guess

The test makers are crafty. Sometimes they'll throw you an intentionally time-consuming question at the end of a game, possibly one involving a rule change that requires you to backtrack and set up the game all over again. Bear in mind that when this happens, they may not be testing who's smart enough to get the correct answer but rather who's clever enough to skip the killer question to devote their precious time to the next game, with a possible payoff of six or seven new points.

## Always Circle the Questions You Skip

Put a big circle in your test booklet around the number of any question you skip. That way, you know where to go when and if you have the time, and you'll be less likely to fill in your answer sheet incorrectly.

## Always Circle the Answers You Choose

Circle the correct answers in your test booklet but don't transfer the answers to your grid right away. That wastes too much time, particularly if you're doing lots of skipping around. Instead, fill in all the answers to a logic game on your answer sheet after you've finished the game.

## Give Yourself Time for a Final Grid Check

Give yourself enough time for a final check of the grid to make sure you've got an oval filled in for every question in the section. Remember, a blank grid has no chance of earning a point, but a guess does!

## LOGIC GAMES STRATEGY

### Step 1: Consider the Setup

- Discover the situation, the entities involved, the action that you are required to perform, and any limitations to that action.

- Use this information to build a master sketch.

### Step 2: Consider the Rules Individually

- Either enter the rules directly into the master sketch or make a shorthand note about them next to the sketch.

### Step 3: Consider the Rules Together

- Look for any deductions that can be made by combining the rules and enter these deductions into the sketch.

### Step 4: Answer the Questions

- If you get an acceptability question, use the rules to knock off choices one by one. Once you've eliminated four, you can select the last one without taking the time to check it.

- When a question supplies new information, make a copy of the master sketch to be used for that question only. Try to deduce as much as possible before looking at the choices. Once you've found the correct answer, select it without looking at the other choices.

- Don't spend too much time on any one question.

- Learn to spot the easy questions and do them first.

Congratulations! By completing this chapter, you are now equipped with the basic tools you need to perform at your best on LSAT Logic Games. If you apply the principles discussed in this lesson—consider the setup and rules, make deductions, and work through the questions systematically—and then combine these principles with a strategic approach to section management, you'll be well on your way to an excellent Logic Games performance on Test Day.

Of all LSAT question types, Logic Games benefit most from practice and as much exposure as possible to the different type of games that can appear on the test. For this reason, be sure to take the post-test at the end of this chapter.

You'll be surprised at how much better your test-taking experience will be as a result of all the hard work you've put into this chapter. Enjoy law school and good luck on Test Day!

# PRACTICE SET

## QUESTIONS 1–5

A band's set list consists of seven songs—"Freebird," "Graceland," "Holiday," "Jump," "Kiss," "Lola," and "Memory." The band is free to play the songs in any order, according to the following conditions:

> "Kiss" is played sometime after "Jump."
> "Graceland" is played exactly two songs before "Holiday."
> "Lola" is played sometime before "Graceland."
> "Kiss" is played either fifth or sixth.
> "Freebird" is played second.

1. Which one of the following sequences would make for an acceptable set?

   A. "Jump," "Freebird," "Lola," "Memory," "Graceland," "Kiss," "Holiday"

   B. "Jump," "Freebird," "Memory," "Graceland," "Kiss," "Holiday," "Lola"

   C. "Lola," "Freebird," "Graceland," "Jump," "Kiss," "Holiday," "Memory"

   D. "Lola," "Freebird," "Jump," "Kiss," "Graceland," "Memory," "Holiday"

   E. "Lola," "Graceland," "Jump," "Holiday," "Kiss," "Freebird," "Memory"

2. Which one of the following is a complete and accurate list of the positions in which "Holiday" can be played?

   A. Fifth, sixth

   B. Fourth, fifth, sixth

   C. Fifth, sixth, seventh

   D. Third, fifth, sixth, seventh

   E. Third, fourth, fifth, sixth, seventh

3. If "Kiss" is the fifth song played, then which one of the following must be true?

    A. "Graceland" is the third song played.

    B. "Holiday" is the fourth song played.

    C. "Jump" is the third song played.

    D. "Lola" is the first song played.

    E. "Memory" is the seventh song played.

4. Which one of the following would make it possible to determine the exact ordering of the songs?

    A. "Graceland" is the fourth song played.

    B. "Holiday" is the fifth song played.

    C. "Kiss" is the sixth song played.

    D. "Lola" is the first song played.

    E. "Memory" is the seventh song played.

5. If "Kiss" is the sixth song played, then which one of the following CANNOT be true?

    A. "Graceland" is the fifth song played.

    B. "Holiday" is the seventh song played.

    C. "Jump" is the fifth song played.

    D. "Lola" is the third song played.

    E. "Memory" is the first song played.

## QUESTIONS 6–10

An art installation consists of two rows of five evenly spaced cups, one row directly above the other. Some cups contain water, and some do not. The first cup in each row is made of ginkgo wood, the second in each is made of birch wood, the third in each is made of rose wood, the fourth in each is made of willow wood, and the fifth in each is made of yew wood. The cups are arranged as follows:

**Top row:** ginkgo, birch, rose, willow, yew
**Bottom row:** ginkgo, birch, rose, willow, yew

The following conditions apply:

The top ginkgo cup is full.
The bottom birch cup is empty.
The bottom rose cup is full.
The top yew cup is empty.

6. If no two cups of the same type of wood are both full, then which of the following must be true?

   A. At least two of the cups in the top row are full.

   B. At least three of the cups in the bottom row are empty.

   C. At least three cups on the panel are full.

   D. The bottom willow cup is empty.

   E. At least five cups on the panel are empty.

7. If exactly two cups in the top row are full, and if every cup in the top row that is empty is directly above a cup that is full, then all of the following must be true EXCEPT

   A. the bottom willow cup is full.

   B. the top rose cup is empty.

   C. the bottom ginkgo cup is empty.

   D. the top birch cup is full.

   E. the bottom yew cup is full.

8. If exactly one cup in the bottom row is full, and if no two adjacent cups in the top row are empty, then which of the following must be true?

   A. If both of the rose cups are full, then neither of the birch cups is full.

   B. If neither of the birch cups is full, then both of the rose cups are full.

   C. If only one of the rose cups is full, then neither of the birch cups is full.

   D. If one of the birch cups is full, then only one of the rose cups is full.

   E. More than one cup in the top row is empty.

9. If exactly one of the willow cups is full, and if no two adjacent cups in a row are full, then which of the following must be true?

   A. The top rose cup is empty.

   B. The top birch cup is full.

   C. Exactly one cup in the bottom row is full.

   D. Exactly two cups in the bottom row are full.

   E. Exactly three cups in the bottom row are full.

10. If at least two adjacent cups in each row are full, and no two adjacent cups in a row are empty, then which of the following CANNOT be true?

    A. The top birch cup is empty.

    B. The top rose cup is full.

    C. The bottom ginkgo cup is full.

    D. The bottom willow cup is empty.

    E. The bottom yew cup is empty.

## QUESTIONS 11–16

A high school principal must select five people to write commencement speeches. The five people will be selected from a group of five graduating seniors—H, I, J, K, and L—and a group of four teachers—q, r, s, and t. The principal's selections must conform to the following conditions:

> At least two people from each group must be selected to write speeches.
> If r is selected to write a speech, neither H nor t can be selected.
> If either J or L is selected to write a speech, the other must also be selected.
> If either I or K is selected to write a speech, the other must also be selected.

11. Who of the following could be the five people selected to write speeches?

    A. H, I, K, q, r

    B. H, J, L, q, t

    C. I, J, K, L, s

    D. I, L, q, s, t

    E. K, L, r, s, t

12. If r is selected to write a speech, whom of the following must also be selected?

    A. H

    B. I

    C. J

    D. s

    E. t

13. Which one of the following pairs of people CANNOT both be selected?

    A. H and t

    B. I and r

    C. J and K

    D. q and r

    E. r and s

14. If H is selected to write a speech, which one of the following must be false?

    A. I is selected to write a speech.

    B. L is selected to write a speech.

    C. t is selected to write a speech.

    D. Exactly two graduating seniors are selected to write speeches.

    E. Exactly two teachers are selected to write speeches.

15. All of the following could be true EXCEPT

    A. both H and J are selected to write speeches.

    B. both I and r are selected to write speeches.

    C. both r and s are selected to write speeches.

    D. neither H nor I are selected to write speeches.

    E. neither q nor s are selected to write speeches.

16. If exactly three teachers are selected to write speeches, which one of the following must be true?

    A. H is selected to write a speech.

    B. J is selected to write a speech.

    C. s is selected to write a speech.

    D. r is selected to write a speech.

    E. t is selected to write a speech.

## QUESTIONS 17–23

For a family portrait, seven members of the Ellis family—Feisal, Gillian, Helen, Ian, Jeremy, Khalia, and Laura—stand in positions numbered one through seven from left to right, according to the following conditions:

Feisal and Gillian do not stand next to each other.
Exactly two people stand between Helen and Feisal.
Ian and Feisal stand next to each other.
Khalia and Gillian do not stand next to each other.
Helen's position is exactly two places to the left of Gillian's position.

17. Which one of the following is an acceptable arrangement of family members from left to right?

   A. Feisal, Ian, Helen, Jeremy, Gillian, Laura, Khalia

   B. Feisal, Ian, Khalia, Helen, Jeremy, Gillian, Laura

   C. Feisal, Khalia, Ian, Gillian, Jeremy, Helen, Laura

   D. Jeremy, Feisal, Ian, Laura, Helen, Khalia, Gillian

   E. Khalia, Jeremy, Ian, Feisal, Gillian, Laura, Helen

18. If Laura stands in position one, then Jeremy must stand

   A. between Gillian and Helen.

   B. between Ian and Laura.

   C. next to Feisal.

   D. next to Khalia.

   E. in position seven.

19. If Laura stands next to Feisal, which one of the following CANNOT be true?

   A. Gillian stands in position seven.

   B. Ian stands in position one.

   C. Ian stands between Feisal and Khalia.

   D. Jeremy stands between Helen and Ian.

   E. Laura stands between Feisal and Khalia.

20. If Jeremy stands in position seven, how many people stand between Jeremy and Laura?

    A. None

    B. One

    C. Two

    D. Four

    E. Five

21. If Ian and Jeremy stand next to each other, how many people stand between Laura and Khalia?

    A. None

    B. One

    C. Two

    D. Four

    E. Six

22. If Laura stands next to Khalia, how many people stand between Gillian and Jeremy?

    A. None

    B. One

    C. Two

    D. Three

    E. Four

23. Which one of the following CANNOT be true?

    A. Feisal stands next to both Ian and Laura.

    B. Gillian stands next to both Jeremy and Laura.

    C. Jeremy stands next to both Gillian and Helen.

    D. Khalia stands next to both Feisal and Laura.

    E. Laura stands next to both Feisal and Jeremy.

# ANSWERS AND EXPLANATIONS

## ANSWER KEY

| | | | |
|---|---|---|---|
| 1. A | 7. C | 13. C | 19. D |
| 2. C | 8. B | 14. D | 20. B |
| 3. E | 9. A | 15. E | 21. D |
| 4. B | 10. D | 16. C | 22. A |
| 5. C | 11. B | 17. B | 23. E |
| 6. E | 12. D | 18. A | |

## BAND'S SET GAME (QUESTIONS 1–5)

### Step 1: Consider the Setup

In this sequencing game, you're asked to put seven songs in order.

### Step 2: Consider the Rules Individually

The natural way to picture this is to write seven slots, or simply write 1 through 7 across the page. As you work with each rule, try to find a way to build each rule into the sketch. K must be played after J. G is played two songs before H. L must be played before G. K is played either fifth or sixth, and F is played second. Rule 5 is concrete, so put it right in the picture.

### Step 3: Combine the Rules

Note that rules 1 and 4 mention the same entity, and rules 2 and 3 mention the same entity, which makes them ripe for combining. After you've combined rules, your scratch work should convey the information concisely, as we've done here:

```
    1   2   3   4   5   6   7
        F               K or K

            L...G__H
            J...K
```

There are quite a few restrictions on the entities, so it's worth the time to consider the implications. What can go last? F is set at second, K is fifth or sixth, J is played sometime before K, G cannot be sixth or seventh, and L must be before G. Therefore, there are only two entities left that can be played seventh: H or M. Similarly, F, K, G, and H cannot go first, so it has to be J, L, or M, the floater. Also recognize that because L must come before G, the soonest that G can be played is third; thus, H can only be fifth, sixth, or seventh. Expect one or more questions that turn on the fact that H and K are basically competing for the same spots. Now that you've taken the time to think thoroughly through the important implications, you should be all set to rack up some points.

### 1. (A)

Here's an acceptable arrangement question, so grab each rule and see which choices violate that rule. Rule 1, placing J before K, doesn't eliminate any choices. However, rule 2, which places G two songs before H, eliminates **(C)**. If you misunderstood rule 2 and thought that two songs had to be between G and H (G _ _ H), then you would have eliminated every choice EXCEPT three, which should have instantly told you that you couldn't have read the rule correctly, because one rule never eliminates every wrong choice on an LSAT acceptable arrangement question. According to rule 3, L is served before G, which eliminates **(B)**. Rule 4 places K fifth or sixth, eliminating **(D)**, and rule 5 places F second, so **(E)** must be wrong. You're left with **(A)**, the correct answer.

### 2. (C)

We saw up front that the earliest G can be played is third, and because G is two places to the left of H, the earliest H can be is fifth. Cross off any choice that has H earlier than fifth: **(B)**, **(D)**, and **(E)**. Now, can H actually play fifth, sixth, or seventh or just fifth and sixth? Well, if we place H seventh, then G would be fifth, and K must be sixth. That leaves J, L and M to go first, third, and fourth, in any order. Therefore, **(C)** is correct.

### 3. (E)

If K is fifth, where can we fit the "G _ H" block? G can't be third because that would require H to be fifth. G can't be sixth or seventh (nowhere for H to go), so G must be fourth and H sixth. We deduced up front that H or M must always be seventh, so here M must be seventh. **(E)** must be true and is the answer. If you didn't make the upfront deduction that either M or H must be seventh, then you had a longer road ahead of you. In this scenario, we're left with this arrangement: _ F _ G K H _. J must be played before K, and L must be played before G. Therefore, between them, J and L must occupy the first and the third positions, although we don't know their order. Regardless, there's only one space left for M, and that's seventh.

### 4. (B)

It would be very clever of you to use your previous work on this one. In question 3, we had G fourth, K fifth, H sixth, and M seventh, but the ordering was not determined (we didn't know exactly when J or L could be played). Therefore, you can eliminate **(A)** and **(E)**. From there, you have to try out each choice. If H is fifth, G must be third (rule 2) and K must be sixth (rule 4). We deduced up front that either H or M must be seventh, so here M must be seventh. L must be before G, and the only open spot before G is 1. J is left to fill in the remaining fourth spot. Everything is determined, so **(B)** is the answer.

### 5. (C)

If K is sixth, then the "G _ H" block could go third-fifth or fifth-seventh. This eliminates **(A)** and **(B)**. It also tells us that **(C)** is correct, because the fifth slot must be taken by either G or H. Again, don't check the other choices unless this is the first game on the test and you need to make absolutely sure you don't make a silly mistake.

## ART INSTALLATION GAME (QUESTIONS 6–10)

### Step 1: Consider the Setup

Here the entities are ten cups in two rows, but it's not a sequence game in as much as the sequence is already given to you. Thus, your job is not to arrange the cups, but rather to keep track of which cups are full and which are empty.

### Step 2: Consider the Rules Individually

It seems that circling and crossing out cups will allow you to keep track of each new cause and effect. You could also draw up a chart with boxes to keep track of what's full and what's empty.

## Step 3: Combine the Rules

Doing it the first way, your master sketch looks like this:

It's worth noticing that the rules are surprisingly quiet in terms of what must be true. For instance, there's no rule about the total number of cups that have to be full or empty at any given time. You know about four of the ten cups but can infer nothing about the other six.

### 6. (E)

If no two cups of the same color are full, then both the bottom G and top R cups are empty. Furthermore, while you can't be entirely sure what's going on with the two W cups, they cannot both be full (for the same reason). Thus, you can be certain that at least three empty cups (one G, one R, and one W) will be present along with the two empty cups specified originally. That makes (E) the correct answer. Contrary to both choices (A) and (C), it's possible that the only full cups are the two originally full. On the other hand, the bottom-row W and Y could be full along with the original R, making (B) incorrect as well. Finally, one of the W's must be empty, but you cannot be sure that it is the bottom-row W, so (D) is wrong.

### 7. (C)

You cannot do anything with the first bit of new information by itself because B, R, or W could be the other full cup. However, taking the second part, if a top row cup is empty, then its same-colored partner in the bottom row is full. Because you know the top-row Y is always empty, the bottom-row Y must be full, making (E) something that must be true and hence a wrong answer here. That's not all we can deduce, though. The contrapositive of this rule is that for every cup on the bottom that is empty, the cup directly above it must be full. That means top B must be full. If it were empty, then the cup below it must be full, and that violates what we know from the starting conditions. Now everything else on top must be empty (R and W) and the cups below them must be full (we already knew R, but we can add W). The only thing that we haven't fixed is bottom G. It could be full or empty. (C) says bottom G is empty, which is not necessarily true.

## 8. (B)

Because the bottom-row R is always full, that's the cup the stem must be referring to, so you can cross out the rest of the row. Also, you know that the top-row W, which is adjacent to the empty Y, must be full, according to the second hypothetical. The story so far:

Ⓖ  B  R  Ⓦ  X̶
X̶  X̶  Ⓡ  W̶  X̶

At this point, you can deal with the choices, and you can see that (B) must be true: if both Bs are empty, both Rs are full. That would have to be the case to avoid adjacent turned-empty cups in the top row. (A) could be false—the stem doesn't forbid adjacent cups being full, just their being empty, so with both Rs full, perhaps the top-row B is full and perhaps it isn't. If it is full, incidentally, then every cup in the top row except Y would be full, indicating that choices four and five need not be true. In addition, (C) is definitely false, because the "only one R" it speaks of must be the one in the bottom row that's always full and if the top-row R is empty, then the top-row B must be full to avoid adjacent turned-empty top-row cups.

## 9. (A)

Seeing as you can have no two adjacent cups full in this question, you can turn empty the cups adjacent to those already full:

Ⓖ  X̶  R  W  X̶
G  X̶  Ⓡ  W̶  Y

Because one willow cup is full, it's got to be the top one, so you can empty one more cup for sure:

Ⓖ  X̶  R̶  Ⓦ  X̶
G  X̶  Ⓡ  W̶  Y

(A) is confirmed as the correct answer. (B) must be false, and you can't determine which of the options identified by choices (C), (D), and (E) must be true.

## 10. (D)

Because you can have no two adjacent cups empty in this question, you can fill the cups adjacent to those already empty. We also have to make sure at least two adjacent cups are full in each row. The only way to do that in the bottom row is to fill the bottom W. Therefore we have this:

That means what **(D)** says is false, because it tells us the bottom W is empty.

# COMMENCEMENT SPEECH WRITERS' GAME (QUESTIONS 11–17)

## Step 1: Consider the Setup

**Situation:** Commencement speech selection

**Entities:** Seniors (H, I, J, K, L) and teachers (q, r, s, t)

**Action:** Grouping

**Limitations:** Select five out of nine

The key issues of this game will involve our typical grouping concerns:

1. What people are selected to write speeches?

2. What seniors can, must, or cannot be selected?

3. What teachers can, must, or cannot be selected?

## Master Sketch

Keep this very simple. Because you're selecting a group of five people, a roster of the available choices as well as five dashes to represent the five positions will work.

SENIORS                    TEACHERS

H I J K L                   q̷ r s t

_____  _____  _____  _____  _____

## Step 2: Consider the Rules Individually

**Rule 1:** You can build this rule into the master sketch. Label two dashes as seniors and two as teachers. The remaining dash may be either a senior or teacher.

**Rule 2:** Remember to separate two-part rules and work with the parts individually. These two if-then statements and their contrapositives tell us that there will never be an rH or rt combination in our picture. Don't make the mistake of inferring a relationship between H and t. You cannot deduce that H and t must or cannot be together.

**Rule 3:** J and L must be selected together or not selected at all.

**Rule 4:** I and K must be selected together or not selected at all.

## Step 3: Combine the Rules

Remember to keep your eyes open for the numbers aspect of Logic Games, especially in grouping games. In this game, you know that at least two seniors and two teachers are selected (rule 1). This means that only two senior-teacher breakdowns are acceptable: either three seniors and two teachers or two seniors and three teachers.

With this limitation in mind, look at the rules again. Rules 3 and 4 give us pairs of seniors that cannot be broken up: JL and IK. Because the maximum number of seniors to be selected is three, we know that these two pairs cannot be selected together. Notice also that H is the only senior who is not a member of a preset pair. That means that if three seniors are chosen, one of these pairs must be chosen along with H.

Because H cannot appear with r (courtesy of rule 2), we also know that if three seniors are chosen, r will not be chosen.

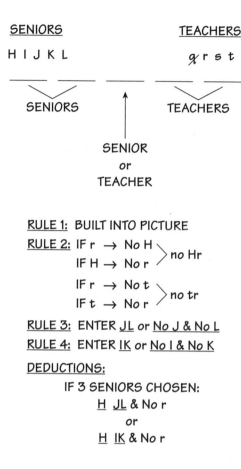

SENIORS                    TEACHERS

H I J K L                    q̶ r s t

_____ _____ _____ _____ _____

   ⌣    ↑    ⌣

 SENIORS       TEACHERS

SENIOR
or
TEACHER

RULE 1: BUILT INTO PICTURE

RULE 2: IF r → No H ⟩ no Hr
          IF H → No r

          IF r → No t ⟩ no tr
          IF t → No r

RULE 3: ENTER <u>JL</u> or <u>No J & No L</u>

RULE 4: ENTER <u>IK</u> or <u>No I & No K</u>

DEDUCTIONS:
    IF 3 SENIORS CHOSEN:
        H  <u>JL</u> & No r
           or
        H  <u>IK</u> & No r

Always take the time to think before you rush into the questions. Not every game will have a "Big Deduction," but most games will reveal important consequences and limitations that need to be considered when you stop to evaluate the rules. For example, the three-senior maximum rule has consequences that can make the question set easier to manage. This extra thinking helps to cement your understanding of the game and lets you quickly cut through many of the questions and wrong answer choices.

You could go further in working out different possibilities, but that really is not necessary. We've gone as far as we need to get a good, solid grasp on the game's workings.

### 11. (B)

This is an acceptability question, so use the rules to eliminate choices. Rule 1 is violated by **(C)**, which picks four seniors and only one teacher. Rule 2 eliminates **(A)** and **(E)**. **(D)** violates rule 3 by including an L without a J. The only choice remaining is **(B)**.

### 12. (D)

Rule 2 tells us that if r is selected, then neither H nor t can be selected, so eliminate **(A)** and **(E)**. Because H cannot be selected, we know that two seniors and three teachers must be chosen (a key deduction made at the outset). Those three teachers must be r (from the question stem), q, and s. Remember, rule 2 will not allow us to choose t. Scanning the answer choices then, you find that **(D)** is s and your right answer.

When there are two possible right answers (such as s and q in this question), only one will show up in the answer choices.

If you took the time to make deductions before getting into the questions, it really would have paid off here. Knowing the student-teacher number combinations made this question easier to handle.

### 13. (C)

Again, think about the deductions we made before getting into the questions. Because the maximum number of seniors that can be selected is three, we know that the pairs of seniors set up by the rules (JL and IK) can never be combined (that would make four seniors—which cannot happen). So any choice that combines one entity from JL with one entity from IK must be false and is, therefore, your right answer. **(C)** combines J with K.

If you couldn't piece together the deduction here, don't worry. You can always check each answer choice. That will take more time but will still earn you the same point.

### 14. (D)

A quick scan of the answer choices tells you that two of the choices are concerned with the numbers of seniors and teachers selected. We deduced at the beginning that H is a key player in determining those numbers. Remember, if H is selected, then three seniors and two teachers are selected (and r cannot be one of the teachers—rule 2). Because the question stem is asking you to identify the false answer choice, **(D)** fits the bill.

## 15. (E)

This non-if question gives us no new information, so we should look for the choice that must be false (the one that violates the rules). Going through the choices, all the combinations work except **(E)**. If neither q nor s give speeches, then the remaining two teachers, r and t, must give speeches to satisfy rule 1's requirement of at least two of each type of speaker. Rule 2, however, forbids this combination of r and t, so **(E)** is the answer.

## 16. (C)

Who could be the three teachers selected? Both r and t cannot be selected (rule 2), so either r or t must be selected with both q and s (either "r q s" or "t q s"). Therefore, both q and s must be selected if three teachers are selected. **(C)** selects s, so it is your answer.

# FAMILY PORTRAIT GAME (QUESTION 17–23)

## Step 1: Consider the Setup

**Situation:** Family portrait

**Entities:** Family members (F, G, H, I, J, K, L)

**Action:** Sequence (the family members into a line)

**Limitations:** Seven people, seven slots, each person used once

**Master Sketch**

This sequencing game requires a very simple sketch. The scenario lines up the family in seven positions numbered 1 through 7 from left to right. That's your sketch. Remember, when your picture is just a simple set of slots, you can create a running grid of your sketch to save time and space.

F G H I J K L

| 1 | 2 | 3 | 4 | 5 | 6 | 7 |
|---|---|---|---|---|---|---|
|   |   |   |   |   |   |   |
|   |   |   |   |   |   |   |
|   |   |   |   |   |   |   |
|   |   |   |   |   |   |   |
|   |   |   |   |   |   |   |

## Step 2: Consider the Rules Individually

**Rule 1:** No FG or GF

**Rule 2:** Must H_ _ F or F_ _ H

**Rule 3:** Must IF or FI

**Rule 4:** No KG or GK

**Rule 5:** H_G (Be careful with rules like this. The normal reaction is to put two spaces between H and G. The safest approach is to start with G and count two spaces to the left for H.)

## Step 3: Combine the Rules

Combine the two possibilities from rule 2 with rule 5. If H appears before F, then the rules combine to give us H_GF, which violates rule 1. The only acceptable way to combine rules 2 and 5 is to use the F_ _H lineup from rule 2. The resulting lineup would be F_ _ H_G. This accounts for six of the seven slots in our sketch. We know that the additional slot will either appear before F or after G.

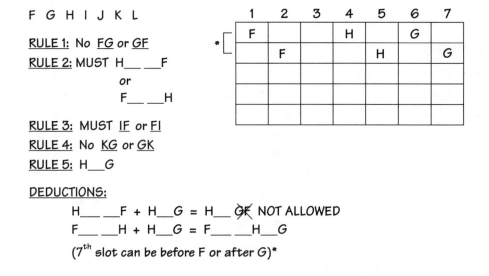

F G H I J K L

RULE 1: No FG or GF

RULE 2: MUST H___ ___F
or
F___ ___H

RULE 3: MUST IF or FI
RULE 4: No KG or GK
RULE 5: H___G

| | 1 | 2 | 3 | 4 | 5 | 6 | 7 |
|---|---|---|---|---|---|---|---|
| | F | | | H | | G | |
| | | F | | | H | | G |
| | | | | | | | |
| | | | | | | | |
| | | | | | | | |

DEDUCTIONS:
  H___ ___F + H___G = H___ ~~GF~~ NOT ALLOWED
  F___ ___H + H___G = F___ ___H___G
  (7th slot can be before F or after G)*

## 17. (B)

Start by eliminating wrong answer choices because they violate the rules. Rule 1 knocks out **(E)**, which has F and G together. Rule 2 eliminates **(A)** and **(C)**. Rule 4 is violated by **(D)** which puts K and G together. That leaves **(B)**, the correct answer.

## 18. (A)

With L in position 1, we know that the lineup we deduced up front will round out the seven slots: LF_ _H_G. The three entities that will fill the remaining slots are I, J, and K. Consult the rules to determine where I, J, and K could be. Rule 3 puts I into position 3. Rule 4 puts K into position 4 (because K can't be next to G). That leaves J in position 6 for the final lineup of LFIKHJG.

The question asks where J must stand. Consult your picture, and you'll find J in position 6 between H and G, **(A)**.

## 19. (D)

L can stand next to F in two positions, either before or after F. Whichever spot L takes, I will take the other to fulfill rule 3's mandate. Either way, J takes position 6 because K cannot be next to G (rule 4). That leaves K in position 4.

The question asks you which of the choices cannot be true under these circumstances, so evaluate the choices.

**(A)** must be true in both scenarios, so you can eliminate **(A)**.

**(B)** could be true. I is in position 1 in the second scenario. Therefore, you can eliminate **(B)**.

**(C)** could be true. I is between F and K in scenario 1, so you can eliminate **(C)**.

**(D)** cannot be true. In both scenarios, J stands between H and G. This is the correct answer.

**(E)** could be true. L is between F and K in scenario 2, so you can eliminate **(E)**.

When a question's hypothetical allows for more than one possibility, be sure to consider all of the acceptable possibilities when answering the question.

**20. (B)**

With J in position 7, F must be in position 1, giving us F_ _H_GJ. Use the rules to round out the lineup. Rule 3 puts I in position 2. Rule 4 puts K in position 3. L, the only entity left, is in position 5. The resulting lineup is FIKHLGJ.

The question asks for the number of people between J and L. Only G is between J and L, so **(B)** is the correct answer.

**21. (D)**

To put I and J next to one another and still have I next to F (Rule 3), I needs to be between F and J. Because there is only room for one entity before F, we know that these three entities must appear in the order FIJ. The lineup thus far is FIJH_G. The seventh entity will appear either before F or after G. Because Rule 4 won't allow G and K next to one another, the remaining slot must be before F and be filled with K. That leaves L for the spot between H and G. The resulting lineup is KFIJHLG.

The question asks for the number of people between L and K. F, I, J, and H stand between L and K, so the answer is **(D)**, four people.

**22. (A)**

The only available space for LK or KL is the pair of spaces between F and H. This forces I into position 1 (rule 3) and J into position 6, between H and G.

The question asks for the number of people between G and J. Because J is next to G, the answer is **(A)**, none.

**23. (E)**

This question is an excellent opportunity to use your previous work. Because this is a non-if question, we have no new information and must tackle the choices one by one. Remember that we're looking for the answer choice that cannot be true.

**(A)** can be true—we saw F between I and L in question 19—So eliminate it.

**(B)** can be true because we saw G between J and L in question 17. Therefore, you can eliminate **(B)**.

(**C**) can be true because we saw J between G and H in question 17. Therefore, you can eliminate (**C**).

(**D**) can be true because we saw K could be between F and L in question 22.

Using your previous work speeds you up on questions like this when you need to evaluate each of the choices.

Remember that the correct answer to an acceptability question always yields an acceptable possibility that can be used to gauge answer choices on later questions.

# CHAPTER 3: **LOGICAL REASONING**

This chapter explores the different kinds of questions you'll encounter on the two LSAT Logical Reasoning sections and introduces a strategic approach to attacking those questions. You'll learn the importance of understanding the basic components of an argument—evidence, conclusion, and assumptions. This is the first step to mastering LSAT Logical Reasoning. The second step is to understand what you are best at and play to those strengths. Let's get started!

## INTRODUCTION TO LOGICAL REASONING

Logical Reasoning questions account for roughly one half of your LSAT score. These questions require you to understand how an argument is structured and how the individual pieces of an argument fit together. In terms of generating your scaled score on the LSAT, there is no question type that is more essential than Logical Reasoning.

Each Logical Reasoning question refers to a short passage that precedes it. The question will require you to analyze the structure and logic of the argument and determine which of the five answer choices best answers the question.

One key thing to remember about the LSAT is that it is a highly predictable test, and the Logical Reasoning sections of the test are no exception. The frequency of the various types of Logical Reasoning questions is very consistent from test to test. Use this predictability to focus your preparation.

Three of the four most common Logical Reasoning questions involve isolating the components of an argument and finding its assumptions. Assumptions, strengthen/weaken, and logical flaw questions comprise roughly one half of all LR questions. The other common question type is inferences questions, which test your ability to make logical deductions based on the information you are given in a stimulus.

The remaining question types tend to focus more on the structure of an argument than its content. Keep in mind that some of these questions (parallel reasoning, in particular) can take quite a bit of time. Because all questions have an equal impact on your final score, a strategic test taker will save the most time-consuming questions for the end of the exam.

# ANATOMY OF A LOGICAL REASONING QUESTION

Below is a typical LSAT Logical Reasoning question along with its directions.

**Directions:** The questions in this section are based on the reasoning contained in brief statements or passages. For some questions, more than one of the answer choices could conceivably answer the question. Your task, however, is to choose the best answer; that is, the most clear and accurate response to the question. You should avoid making assumptions that are by commonsense standards implausible, superfluous, or incompatible with the passage. After you have chosen the best answer, blacken the corresponding oval on your answer sheet.

A recent study has concluded that, contrary to the claims of those trying to ban cigarette advertisements altogether, cigarette ads placed on billboards and in magazines have little to no effect on the smoking habits of the smokers who view the ads. The study, which surveyed more than 20,000 smokers and solicited their reasons for continuing to smoke, found that practically no one in the survey felt that these advertisements influenced their decision to smoke.

The study's conclusion is based upon which of the following assumptions?

    A. People do not switch cigarette brands based on their exposure to cigarette ads on billboards and in magazines.

    B. Cigarette ads on billboards and in magazines do not encourage nonsmokers to take up the habit.

    C. Banning cigarette advertisements altogether will encourage people to give up smoking.

    D. People are consciously aware of all the reasons they choose to smoke

    E. People who decide to smoke do so for rational reasons.

## BREAKING IT DOWN

Here's a breakdown of all the parts of the Logical Reasoning stimulus and question.

### The Directions

The directions are wordier than they need to be. For instance, you can disregard that business about "one or more of the choices could conceivably answer the question"— that's just a bit of legalese thrown in by the test makers to forestall any possible challenges to the test. In fact, each of the four wrong answer choices to a Logical Reasoning question contains something that makes it wrong.

Some of what it says here should be reassuring, however. For instance, while it might seem as if you need an education in formal logic to do well in this section, applying commonsense standards is generally sufficient to answer these questions.

### The Stimulus

This is a short passage, typically in the form of an argument, which may be drawn from many possible areas, including the natural sciences, the humanities, law, and even casual conversation. Even if the subject matter seems strange, relax. All the information you need to answer the question is on the page. You don't need to bring in any outside knowledge.

### The Question

Read the question *first!* Here's where you find out your task. You may need to identify an argument's assumption or flaw, you may need to determine what would strengthen or weaken the argument, or you may be asked to make a deduction. Pay close attention here: if you misinterpret the question, all your other work will go to waste.

### The Answer Choices

The test makers have set up one (and only one) of these choices to be correct. If you understand the question and are able to follow the argument, you should be able to zero in on the correct answer quickly. Wrong answer choices usually distort the text, misrepresent its scope, or are the opposite of what you're looking for.

# ATTACKING LOGICAL REASONING STRATEGICALLY

## KAPLAN'S 5-STEP METHOD FOR LOGICAL REASONING QUESTIONS

**Step 1: Read the question stem first.** When you first encounter a Logical Reasoning question, decide quickly whether to do it now or later. Read the question stem first to see if it is a question type you feel comfortable tackling at this time. Play to your own strengths. Some questions take a good deal of time to answer, while others can be handled within a minute or so. Understanding yourself as a test taker and playing to your strengths is the key to significant score improvements on the LSAT.

**Step 2: Use the information in the question stem to focus your attack on the stimulus.** Different question types require slightly different approaches. Quite a few questions require you to look for an argument's key assumptions. Others will require you to make inferences based on the information you have been given. Still others will ask you to understand the structure, or method, to an argument. Regardless, the question stem will give you invaluable clues that will focus your attack on the stimulus.

**Step 3: Attack the stimulus.** On assumption, strengthen/weaken, and flaw questions, isolate the conclusion (the author's main point) and the evidence (the support the author provides for that point). Identify any assumptions (unstated, yet necessary premises) that fill in gaps between the evidence and conclusion. On inference questions, a paraphrase of the argument is most helpful. For method of argument or parallel reasoning questions, a sense of the overall structure of the argument is what you are reading for.

> **STRATEGY TIP**
> The brief passages you will encounter in the Logical Reasoning sections of the LSAT are frequently referred to as *arguments*. This doesn't mean that the test maker is disagreeable; it just means that these passages, or stimuli, are attempting to convince or persuade you of something. Understanding and identifying the three main components of an argument is one of the best things you can do to improve your performance in Logical Reasoning.

**Step 4: Whenever possible, predict the answer before you examine the answer choices.** This saves you time and prevents you from falling prey to trap answer choices. However, for inference and parallel reasoning questions, coming up with a prediction might not be so easy. In these cases, proceed directly to the answer choices.

**Step 5: Attack the answer choices.** Read the answer choices and choose the one that comes closest to your prediction. A quick scan for a match of your prediction can save valuable time over reading through and evaluating each choice. Avoid choices that use extreme language or are outside the scope of the argument. When stuck, evaluate choices, eliminate obviously incorrect answers, take a guess, and move on.

Let's examine the structure of arguments.

# UNDERSTANDING ARGUMENTS

## EVIDENCE AND CONCLUSIONS

On the LSAT, an argument is an attempt to persuade you to accept its conclusion through the use of evidence. To understand an LSAT argument, you must be able to locate and identify these parts within the passage.

When attacking an argument, first ask yourself: What point is the argument trying to make? This main point is the conclusion of the argument. Once you have found the conclusion, ask yourself: What evidence is used to support that claim?

**Breaking Down the Argument**

The following argument is an example of a typical LSAT stimulus and question stem. Take some time to understand the components of an LSAT argument. Each sentence performs a unique role. Think about the function of each component and how you were able to identify that function.

> A recent study has concluded that, contrary to the claims of those trying to ban cigarette advertisements altogether, cigarette ads placed on billboards and in magazines have little to no effect on the smoking habits of the smokers who view the ads. The study, which surveyed more than 20,000 smokers and solicited their reasons for continuing to smoke, found that practically no one in the survey felt that these advertisements influenced their decision to smoke.
>
> The study's conclusion is based upon which of the following assumptions?

Here are explanations of the role each sentence plays within the argument.

**The first sentence is the study's conclusion.** The main point of the study is that smokers were not affected by cigarette ads placed on billboards. The keyword *concluded* indicates the function of this sentence. Look for keywords such as *conclude, must, should, therefore, thus,* and *consequently* when searching for the conclusion of an argument.

**The second sentence is the evidence in this argument.** The evidence here is the survey of 20,000 smokers. Surveys or polls frequently are used as evidence in LSAT arguments.

**The third sentence is the question stem** of this assumption question. Remember always to read the question stem first on LR questions.

Identifying the evidence and conclusion is the key to finding the third and final part of an argument—its assumptions.

## ASSUMPTIONS

Now that we have looked at the two explicitly stated components of an argument, it is time to examine the third and final part—assumptions.

**Definition:** *An assumption is an unstated yet necessary premise to an argument.*

What this means is that an assumption is very much like an unstated piece of evidence. Assumptions must be true for the argument to make logical sense.

Here is a more visual way to understand how arguments are structured:

Evidence + Assumption → Conclusion

Keep in mind, the evidence and conclusions are explicitly stated, while assumptions are not.

## Breaking Down the Argument

Let's take look at another argument:

> All men are mortal.
> Therefore, Socrates is mortal.

Take some time to think about this argument and the assumptions it contains. Here, the evidence is that "All men are mortal." The conclusion (note the keyword *therefore*) is that "Socrates is mortal."

When looking for an argument's assumptions, ask yourself the following two questions:

1. What is not explicitly stated but must be true for the argument to make logical sense?

2. What terms appear in the evidence that do not appear in the conclusion and vice versa?

In response to the first question, *we must assume that Socrates is a man.* Assuming this allows us to link the two statements and allows the argument to make logical sense.

In response to the second question, the term *men* is used in the evidence, while the term *Socrates* is used in the conclusion. A central assumption in this argument will connect the term *Socrates* to the term *men.*

Understanding assumptions also helps with strengthen/weaken questions and faulty logic questions (as we will see later). If we wanted to find fault with this argument, we would attack its central assumption. If Socrates were a cat, a space station, or a woman, the argument would no longer make logical sense. Therefore, for this argument to be valid, one must assume that Socrates is a man and rule out any alternative possibilities.

## Predicting the Assumption

Now let's apply what we know about the structure of arguments to the argument we looked at earlier:

> A recent study has concluded that, contrary to the claims of those trying to ban cigarette advertisements altogether, cigarette ads placed on billboards and in magazines have little to no effect on the smoking habits of the smokers who view the ads. The study, which surveyed more than 20,000 smokers and solicited their reasons for continuing to smoke, found that practically no one in the survey felt that these advertisements influenced their decision to smoke.
>
> The study's conclusion is based upon which of the following assumptions?

We've already isolated the evidence and the conclusion of the argument; they are listed in the following table. Pencil your prediction of the argument's assumption in the box between the evidence and conclusion. Then see how well your prediction matches ours.

| Evidence | Conclusion | Assumption |
|---|---|---|
| Survey of smokers found that practically no one in the survey felt that these ads influenced their decision to smoke. | Cigarette ads placed on billboards and in magazines have little to no effect on the smoking habits of smokers who view the ads. | **Your prediction:** This argument assumes that _____ _____ _____ _____ <br><br> **Our assumption:** This argument assumes that participants in the survey were consciously aware of and would honestly admit to the influence of the ads on their smoking habits. |

## ARGUMENT ASSUMPTION PRACTICE

Now we can see how assumptions are tested on the LSAT itself. Keep in mind the work you did predicting the argument's assumption. For the following two questions, use that prediction to scan the answer choices and find the correct answers quickly and efficiently.

> A recent study has concluded that, contrary to the claims of those trying to ban cigarette advertisements altogether, cigarette ads placed on billboards and in magazines have little to no effect on the smoking habits of the smokers who view the ads. The study, which surveyed more than 20,000 smokers and solicited their reasons for continuing to smoke, found that practically no one in the survey felt that these advertisements influenced their decision to smoke.

1. The study's conclusion is based on which of the following assumptions?

   A. People do not switch cigarette brands based on their exposure to cigarette ads on billboards and in magazines.

   B. Cigarette ads on billboards and in magazines do not encourage nonsmokers to take up the habit.

   C. Banning cigarette advertisements altogether will encourage people to give up smoking.

   D. People are consciously aware of all the reasons they choose to smoke.

   E. People who decide to smoke do so for rational reasons.

**(D)** identifies the key assumption here. If people aren't consciously aware of all of the reasons they choose to smoke, then the fact that those surveyed don't feel that the advertisements influence their decision to smoke does not, in fact, prove that these ads don't affect their smoking habits.

**(A)** is outside the scope of the argument. The argument concerns smokers' decisions to smoke, not which brands they choose once they've decided to smoke.

**(B)** is again outside the scope of the argument. We're concerned with the smoking habits of smokers who view the ads. How nonsmokers react to the ads is of no concern to us.

**(C):** This choice contradicts the argument, which is the opposite of what we're looking for. An assumption should *support* the conclusion.

**(E)** goes way too far. Nothing in the argument implies that people who decide to smoke do so for "rational" reasons.

Let's try another question.

> Biochemical researchers have long questioned why many vertebrates engage in geophagy—the consumption of soil or clay. Scientists have hypothesized that geophagy aids digestion, adds minerals to the diet, and may possibly even remove toxins from other foods through absorption. A recent study of Amazonian parrots indicates that consumption of clay neither aids parrots' digestion nor adds minerals to their diet but does prevent the accumulation of toxins in their bloodstreams. Clearly, the function of geophagy for vertebrates is to aid in the removal of bodily toxins.
>
> 2. The conclusion in the previous argument depends on which of the following assumptions?
>
>    A. All soil- or clay-eating vertebrates derive the same benefit from geophagy.
>
>    B. All vertebrates who engage in geophagy consume soil or clay that is chemically similar to Amazonian clay.
>
>    C. Vertebrates who consume soil or clay have lower concentrations of toxins in their bloodstreams than vertebrates who do not consume soil or clay.
>
>    D. When vertebrates eat soil or clay, their bodies absorb the minerals found in the soil into their bloodstreams.
>
>    E. Soil and clay can irritate and inflame the digestive tracts of animals who consume these substances.

The question stem tells you that you are looking for an assumption. Therefore, you must identify the missing link between the evidence and the conclusion.

**Conclusion:** The keyword *clearly* indicates that the last sentence is the conclusion: geophagy serves the function of removing toxins from vertebrates' diets.

**Evidence:** Scientists have hypothesized that geophagy—or soil eating—may confer a number of benefits on vertebrates who engage in the practice. A study of Amazonian parrots demonstrated that while geophagy did prevent toxins from accumulating in the parrots' bloodstream, it did not confer the other predicted benefits.

Did you notice the shift in scope between the evidence and conclusion? The evidence talks about parrots, while the conclusion talks about all vertebrates. To link the evidence to the conclusion, the author needs to connect the subject discussed in the conclusion—all vertebrates that eat dirt—to the evidence—parrots that eat dirt.

**(A)** makes this connection.

If soil-eating vertebrates consume soil or clay that is *not* chemically similar to the Amazonian clay, the argument is not weakened, because we do not know whether other soil or clay confers similar benefits. Therefore, **(B)** is not correct.

**(C)** is an irrelevant comparison. The stimulus only concerns animals that engage in the practice of geophagy.

**(D)** undermines the conclusion by suggesting another possible benefit from soil eating.

**(E)** raises a negative effect of the behavior, rather than linking the parrots' benefits to other animals who engage in the same behavior. If there are no negative effects, the argument does not fall apart. Therefore, **(E)** is not a necessary assumption.

Now that we've looked at assumption questions, let's move on to other questions that focus on the basic components of an argument.

# STRENGTHEN/WEAKEN QUESTIONS

Strengthen/weaken questions are probably the most common Logical Reasoning questions you'll see, and they can be handled very quickly by identifying the parts of the argument.

When you're asked to strengthen or weaken an argument, take the following two steps:

**Step 1: Break down the argument.** Just as with assumption questions, identify the evidence and conclusion. Then find the author's key assumptions.

**Step 2:** To strengthen an argument, **pick the choice that fills in a key assumption;** to weaken an argument, **pick the choice that denies or undercuts a key assumption.**

To see how this works, apply this technique to the following questions. Then compare your analysis with ours.

## STRENGTHEN/WEAKEN PRACTICE

Let's look at typical strengthen/weaken questions you might see on the LSAT. In the first case, we want to weaken the author's conclusion by attacking the link between the evidence and the conclusion; in the second, we want to strengthen the author's conclusion by reinforcing the link between the evidence and the conclusion.

> Whitley Hospital's much-publicized increase in emergency room efficiency, which its spokespeople credit to new procedures for handling trauma patients, does not withstand careful analysis. The average time before treatment for all patients is nearly 40 minutes—the highest in the city. Furthermore, for trauma victims, who are the specific target of the guidelines, the situation is even worse: the average time before treatment is nearly half an hour—more than twice the city average.

3. Which of the following, if true, would most seriously weaken the conclusion about the value of the new procedures?

   A. The city hospitals with the most efficient emergency rooms utilize the same procedures for handling trauma patients as does Whitley Hospital.

   B. After the new procedures went into effect, Whitley's average time before treatment for trauma patients and patients in general dropped by nearly 35 percent.

   C. Because trauma patients account for a large percentage of emergency room patients, procedures that hasten their treatment will likely increase overall emergency room efficiency.

   D. Due to differences in location and size of staff, not all emergency rooms can be expected to reach similar levels of efficiency.

   E. The recently hired administrators who instituted the new procedures also increased Whitley's emergency room staff by nearly 15 percent.

All of the evidence is intended to show that Whitley's ER moves at a snail's pace and, thus, that efficiency isn't up.

It does not, however, really show this.

Just because Whitley has the slowest ER in the city doesn't mean that Whitley's efficiency hasn't grown by leaps and bounds. Evidence comparing Whitley to other hospitals (which is all the author presents) is irrelevant. What's important is how Whitley's present efficiency compares to its previous efficiency.

If **(B)** is true, then Whitley's efficiency is up, and this seems likely to be the result of the new procedures. Even though it's still the slowest ER around, it's improved markedly.

**(A)**'s claim that these procedures are used in the best ERs does not show that the procedures are good and are, therefore, responsible for the improvements at Whitley. For one thing, the other ERs could be fast for reasons other than the procedures. Furthermore, even if the procedures generally increase efficiency, Whitley's staff could be so incompetent that the procedures are ineffective. The key is information about Whitley's past ER efficiency, not information about other hospitals.

**(C)** is too weak; even if the procedures are intended to speed the treatment of trauma victims (that's not actually said, you notice), there's no reason to assume that they worked at Whitley.

**(D)** might excuse Whitley for offering below-average care, but it gives us no reason to think that Whitley's care has improved, which is what we need.

**(E)** tells us that the new procedures have been accompanied by new administrators and more staff. Therefore, if there has been an increase in efficiency, this complicates things a bit; we wouldn't know exactly what accounted for the increase. The problem, though, is that **(E)** provides no reason to believe that there has been an increase in efficiency.

Let's try another.

*Principal Glasser:* The local high school students have been clamoring for the freedom to design their own curricula. Allowing this would be as disastrous as allowing three-year-olds to choose their own diets. These students have neither the maturity nor the experience to equal that of the professional educators now doing the job.

4. Which of the following statements, if true, would most strengthen Principal Glasser's argument?

   A. High school students have less formal education than those who currently design the curriculum.

   B. The ability to design good curricula develops only after years of familiarity with educational institutions and adult life.

   C. The local high school students are less intelligent than the average teenager.

   D. Individualized curricula are more beneficial to high school students than are the standard curricula, which are needlessly rigid and unresponsive to their particular strengths and weaknesses.

   E. Three-year-olds do not, if left to their own devices, choose healthful diets.

The conclusion here is that allowing students to design their own curricula would be as disastrous as allowing three-year-olds to choose their own diets. The main evidence used to support this claim is that students lack the maturity and experience of the professional educators currently doing the job. Therefore, Principal Glasser's assumption is that maturity and educational experience are necessary for good curriculum design. A good strengthener will solidify this link.

**(B)** does this nicely. It states that only years of familiarity with educational institutions (experience) and adult life (maturity) allow for the ability to design good curricula. This directly links the evidence with the conclusion and is, therefore, the correct answer.

**(A)**'s claim is a mild strengthener, but it is outside the scope of the argument. "Formal education" is not central to the argument, while maturity and experience are central to the principal's claims.

**(C)** makes an irrelevant comparison between local high school students and the average teenager. It does not compare local students with the educators currently designing the curricula, and it does not directly address the evidence (maturity and experience) used by the principal to justify the use of professional educators.

**(D)** is outside the scope of the argument. It does not address why professional educators are best suited to design the high school's curricula. If anything, evidence for the value of more individualized curricula would weaken Principal Glasser's argument.

**(E)** helps establish a minor part of the principal's argument, but it does little to strengthen the connection between the main piece of evidence and the conclusion. The focus of this argument is not on three-year-olds' nutritional knowledge but instead on local high school students' ability to design their own curricula. **(E)** provides reinforcement for a portion of the argument that does not need support.

The strongest choice will link experience and maturity to the ability to design strong curricula. Only **(B)** does this effectively.

Next we will look at the faulty logic and flawed arguments that are the bread and butter of LSAT Logical Reasoning. Most of these arguments require you to do exactly what we've been working on throughout this lesson—isolate the evidence and conclusion of an argument and then identify its assumptions.

# LOGICAL FLAW QUESTIONS

Certain types of flawed arguments appear time and time again. This is because flawed arguments can generate quite a few different types of questions on the LSAT. Flawed arguments are easily strengthened or weakened and often involve large assumptions. Getting comfortable with these typical flaws is one of the keys to mastering Logical Reasoning.

## ALTERNATIVE POSSIBILITIES

The first flaw of this type we will look at involves alternative explanations or possibilities. Faulty arguments of this type claim that one possible explanation to a situation is the one and only explanation to the situation.

Any time you encounter an argument on the LSAT where the author claims that *one of several* possible conclusions is the *only possible* conclusion, watch out for alternative possibilities. Excellent weakeners in arguments of this type point out possible explanations that are different from the conclusion offered by the author.

Here is a very basic example of a flawed argument of this type:

> *My car is not running this morning. Clearly, someone has tampered with it.*

This somewhat paranoid conclusion is only one possible reason why the car is not running. It could be out of gas, it could have a dead battery, or it could be the victim of sabotage. The key idea here is that one of many possible explanations was chosen as the single explanation for the situation at hand. This is a typical flaw that appears throughout the LSAT, especially when the conclusion is introduced with a word such as *clearly*.

Now look for alternative explanations to undermine the following argument:

> Five years ago, in an effort to boost economic development, the country of Liguria slashed its sales tax on gasoline. The high tax had been implemented eight years ago in the hopes of raising revenue, but it was felt that by artificially inflating the price of gasoline, it discouraged the use of automobiles by all but the very rich—in effect, stifling the development of trade and industry in the impoverished country. Since the tax cut, the annual consumption of gasoline in Liguria has tripled. Clearly, many Ligurians who did not previously own cars have decided to buy them.

> 5. Which of the following statements, if true, casts the most doubt on the argument?

>   A. The rise in the consumption of gasoline allowed the Ligurian government's income from the gasoline tax to remain steady, despite the dramatic reduction in the tax rate.

>   B. Following the reduction in the Ligurian gas tax, two foreign car manufacturers opened factories in the country.

>   C. The reduction of the gas tax was part of a comprehensive program introduced by the Ligurian government to stimulate manufacturing and commerce, which included improving the road and highway system.

     D. In the years after the gas tax was cut, those Ligurians who
         owned cars drove them much more often and for longer
         distances than they had before.

     E. Four years after Liguria cut its gas tax, a landslide shut down its
         most important railway line for a period of months.

The conclusion here is that "clearly, many Ligurians who did not previously own cars have decided to buy them." This is based on the evidence that gas consumption has tripled since the gas tax was cut.

This is not, however, the only possible explanation for the increase in gas consumption. Gas consumption could have increased for any number of reasons. A good weakener of this argument would provide another explanation for the increase in gas consumption.

This is exactly what **(D)** does. Rather than assuming that gas consumption increased because more cars were bought, this choice points out the alternative possibility that cars that were already purchased were used more due to the cheaper gas prices.

Of the wrong answer choices, no choice provides a clear-cut alternative explanation of the increase in gas consumption.

**(A)** discusses income from taxes, so it is outside the scope of the question.

**(B)** and **(C)** are outside the scope of the argument because they fail to address directly the increase in gas consumption.

## Scope Shifts

In addition to arguments that are flawed because they fail to allow for alternative explanations, some arguments are flawed due to a subtle shift of scope from the evidence to the conclusion.

Pay close attention to the subject of the evidence and the subject of the conclusion. If a subtle shift or change occurs, the argument must make some assumptions to account for the shift. Frequently these assumptions are flawed.

Following is an example of a flawed argument of this type:

Advertisement: There's nothing on the market that matches the technical sophistication of the Wilkerson dishwasher. On average, Wilkerson dishwashers break down only once every 20 years, while all other dishwashers break down roughly once every 8 years.

Notice the subtle shift here: we went from talking about "technical sophistication" to frequency of breakdowns. The scope has shifted, and this shift allows the argument to be attacked if necessary. A good weakener of this argument would sharpen the distinction between "technical sophistication" and how often a dishwasher breaks down.

Let's try applying this to a practice question. Pay special attention to scope shifts in the following argument:

A team of pediatricians recently announced that dogs are more likely to bite children under age 13 than in any other age group. Their finding was based on a study showing that the majority of all dog bites requiring medical attention involved children under 13. The study also found that the dogs most likely to bite are German shepherds, males, and nonneutered dogs.

6. Which of the following statements, if true, would most weaken the pediatricians' conclusion that dogs are more likely to bite children under 13 than any other age group?

A. More than half of the dog bites not requiring medical attention, which exceeds the number requiring such attention, involve people aged 13 and older.

B. The majority of dog bites resulting in death of the bitten person involve people aged 65 and older.

C. Many serious dog bites affecting children under age 13 are inflicted by female dogs, neutered dogs, and dogs that are not German shepherds.

D. Most dog bites of children under 13 that require medical attention are far less serious than they initially appear.

E. Most parents can learn to treat dog bites effectively if they avail themselves of a small amount of medical information.

The question stem helps focus your attack here. We are looking only at the conclusion that dogs are more likely to bite children under age 13 than any other age group. That conclusion is based on the evidence that "the majority of all bites requiring medical attention involved children under 13." Note the scope shift here. The evidence focuses on dog bites "requiring medical attention," whereas the conclusion claims to represent all dog bites. Consequently, a good weakener will call attention to this shift.

This is exactly what **(A)** does.

**(B)** brings in the idea of dog bites resulting in death, which is outside the scope of the argument.

**(C)** focuses on a conclusion other than the one asked about in the question stem.

**(D)** addresses part of the problem, by focusing on dog bites requiring medical attention, but it fails to relate this to the number of dog bites in general.

**(E)** focuses on an irrelevant distinction about parents of children with dog bites. Choices this far outside the scope can be quickly eliminated.

## CORRELATION VERSUS CAUSATION

The final flaw we will look at involves correlation/causation. Anytime you encounter an argument involving causation on the LSAT, be very careful. Remember that just because two things occur together does not mean that one caused the other. *Correlation does not imply causation.*

Here is an example of a flawed argument of this type:

> *I recently read that the majority of Olympic gold medalists were not married when they won their medals. To increase my chances in next year's Olympics, I think I will divorce my husband.*

In this humorous example, the correlation of gold medals to not being married is confused with a causal relationship—that being single causes Olympic victories. Always be conscious of the distinction between correlation (A and B occur together) and causation (A caused B or B caused A). This error in reasoning appears frequently on the LSAT.

Let's see how this might be tested in a question. Pay special attention to the relevance of the study to the conclusion made by the college student in the following argument. Remember that just because two things occur together, it does not necessarily mean that a causal relationship exists between the two events.

> While reading his psychology textbook, a college sophomore comes across a study showing that intellectuals generally drink wine while nonintellectuals prefer beer. Hoping to do well on his next morning's exam, he goes out and buys a gallon of wine to drink while studying.

> 7. Which one of the following is the major flaw in the student's reasoning?

>   A. He confuses cause and effect in his interpretation of the study.

>   B. He ignores the fact that alcohol destroys brain cells.

>   C. He assumes a causal connection that is not suggested by the study.

>   D. He fails to check the size of the sample used for the study.

>   E. He fails to consider the effect of the previous night's drinking on his abilities the morning of the exam.

The confused sophomore who buys wine in order to do better on the test evidently assumes that wine drinking causes intellectual brilliance. This is a classic case of confusing correlation and causation: he's taken the study's correlation (intellectuals and their preference for wine) and inferred a causal relationship (intellectuals are smart because they drink wine). Be very careful when dealing with causal connections on the LSAT; just because two things are correlated does not mean that one caused the other.

(**C**) is the correct answer here.

(**A**) is tricky but distorts the point. (**A**) says that the sophomore reverses the causality. In other words, (**A**) claims that the study says that being an intellectual causes a preference for wine. While this is an equally unwarranted line of reasoning to that of the sophomore, this is not what the sophomore is doing.

**(B)** discusses a drawback of alcohol use but does nothing to address the flawed reasoning used by the sophomore.

**(D)** brings up the irrelevant issue of the size of the sample.

**(E)** focuses on the effects of drinking but fails to focus on the flawed reasoning involved in making an erroneous conclusion based on the evidence in the study.

# INFERENCE QUESTIONS

Inference questions test your ability to make logical deductions based on the information you are given in a stimulus.

**Definition:** *An inference is a valid deduction from the stimulus (i.e., a statement that must be true if everything in the stimulus is true).*

Inferences are like unstated conclusions. Keep in mind, however, that they may refer only to a small part of an argument.

Let's again take a look at the following argument:

> *All men are mortal.*
> *Socrates is a man.*

What can be inferred from this argument? Without getting too fancy, you can see that you can infer that Socrates is mortal.

Unfortunately, on the LSAT, the inferences you are asked to make are not always so obvious. Nevertheless, one thing is always the case—if the statements in the argument are true, then the inference must also be true.

## PARAPHRASING

When faced with an inference question, begin by paraphrasing the argument (putting the argument in your own words). The correct inference should be consistent with your paraphrase. Paraphrasing and avoiding extreme or sweeping language are the two keys to LSAT inference questions. Then proceed directly to the answer choices and eliminate those that use sweeping or extreme language.

# EXTREME LANGUAGE EXERCISE

On inference questions in particular, and on the LSAT in general, some answer choices are incorrect because of their use of extreme or sweeping language. The following exercise is designed to refresh your memory of extreme versus unbiased language. Most correct answer choices use unbiased language, and many wrong answer choices use extreme language.

Check in the appropriate column whether each the following words is either extreme or unbiased.

| | EXTREME | UNBIASED |
|---|---|---|
| always | | |
| often | | |
| may | | |
| every | | |
| each | | |
| impossible | | |
| might | | |
| suggests | | |
| never | | |
| tend to | | |
| sometimes | | |
| only | | |
| possible | | |
| must | | |
| some | | |
| cannot | | |
| all | | |

**Answers**

|  | EXTREME | UNBIASED |
|---|:---:|:---:|
| always | ✓ |  |
| often |  | ✓ |
| may |  | ✓ |
| every | ✓ |  |
| each | ✓ |  |
| impossible | ✓ |  |
| might |  | ✓ |
| suggests |  | ✓ |
| never | ✓ |  |
| tend to |  | ✓ |
| sometimes |  | ✓ |
| only | ✓ |  |
| possible |  | ✓ |
| must | ✓ |  |
| some |  | ✓ |
| cannot | ✓ |  |
| all | ✓ |  |

## INFERENCES AND FORMAL LOGIC

Some inference questions test your knowledge of formal logic. The key to these questions is noticing either an if-then statement or a disguised if-then statement.

If you see an *only* or an *only if* in an LSAT stimulus, translate that into the *then* part of an if-then statement and look for inferences (contrapositives) from there.

For example, take a look at the following statement:

> It is an historical fact that **only in conditions of profound societal instability** are great works of literature produced.

This can be turned into the following if-then statement. Remember that what follows the *only* becomes what follows the *then*:

> If great works of literature are produced, **then there must be conditions of profound societal instability**.

Therefore, the contrapositive of this statement must also be true:

> If there are no conditions of profound societal instability, then no great works of literature are produced.

To find the contrapositive of an if-then statement, *reverse* the if-then terms and *negate them*. That is, take what follows the *if* in the original statement and put it after the *then* in the contrapositive. Then take what follows the *then* in the original statement and put it after the *if* in the contrapositive. Then negate both terms. In a generalized form, the contrapositive looks like this:

**If A, then B** becomes **If not B, then not A**.

## INFERENCE QUESTION PRACTICE

The number of wild tigers living in India dropped from an estimated 40,000 at the turn of the century to 2,000 in 1970. Although determined conservation efforts have halted the precipitous decline, the survival of the wild tiger in India is uncertain even now. Still, it is beyond doubt that if the tiger is to survive in the wild at all, its best chance is in India.

8. If all of the above statements are true, which one of the following must also be true?

   A. There are now more than 2,000 wild tigers surviving in India.

   B. There are fewer than 2,000 wild tigers living in the wild outside of India.

C. If tigers fail to survive in the wild in India, the species will become extinct.

D. It is impossible for a tiger raised in captivity ever to adapt successfully to life in the wild.

E. The survival of the wild tiger in countries other than India is also endangered.

Inference questions can be difficult to predict, so let's proceed directly to the answer choices. The correct answer will be the choice that must be true, and cannot be false, if the information in the stimulus is all true.

**(A)** states that there are now more than 2,000 wild tigers surviving in India. Is this something we can infer from the stimulus? No, we are told "determined conservation efforts have halted the precipitous decline." However, we do not know that the numbers have increased. We can only infer that numbers are not declining at the same rate as before, not that the numbers have rebounded.

**(B)** states that there are fewer than 2,000 wild tigers living in the wild outside of India. This does not have to be true. We are told that the tigers' best chance of survival is in India, but there could be pockets of several hundred wild tigers scattered all over the globe. In total, there could very easily be more than 2,000 wild tigers outside of India.

**(C)** is too extreme. We are told that the tigers' "best chance" is in India but not that its "only chance" is there. Avoid extreme language on LSAT inference questions.

**(D)** is outside the scope of the argument and uses extreme language. The argument focuses on "wild tigers," while this choice centers around a tiger "raised in captivity." Also, to say that this is "impossible" is extreme and not supported by the passage.

That leaves **(E)**, which is the correct answer. Keep in mind, if you eliminate four choices, the remaining choice must be correct, and you should choose it and move on. The argument states that the wild tiger's "best chance is in India." This means that its survival must be in danger everywhere else. **(E)** also cannot be false. If the wild tiger was not in danger elsewhere, there would be no reason to think that its best chance of survival was in India. Therefore, **(E)** must be correct.

It is an historical fact that only in conditions of profound societal instability are great works of literature produced. During the first century BCE, Rome experienced almost constant civil war accompanied by social upheaval. It wasn't until the ascension of Nerva to the throne in 96 CE that the situation stabilized. Throughout the second century CE, Rome experienced a century of uninterrupted peace and stability.

9.  If all of the statements in the passage are true, which one of the following must also be true?

   A.  During the first century BCE, great works of literature were produced in Rome.

   B.  Roman art of the first century BCE was superior to Roman art of the second century CE.

   C.  During the second century CE, no great works of literature were produced in Rome.

   D.  Historically, great works of literature can stir emotions that find their expression in political action.

   E.  The first century CE was a time of decreased literary production in Rome.

Inference questions involving formal logic are vulnerable to prediction. As we saw before, "only in conditions of profound societal instability are great works of literature produced" translates into "if great works of literature are produced, then there is profound societal instability." The contrapositive of this statement is "if there is no profound societal instability, then no great works of literature are produced."

In terms of the history of Rome, we are told that throughout the second century CE, there was no profound societal instability. Therefore, during the second century CE, no great works of literature were produced in Rome. **(C)** states this nicely.

Notice that **(A)** reverses the previous if-then statement, and you cannot do this. Profound societal instability is necessary for the production of great works of literature, but does not guarantee that they will be produced. All you can infer is that great literature could have been produced in the first century, not that it was in fact produced. An if-then statement produces one and only one logical inference—its contrapositive. Make sure you're comfortable dealing with if-then statements and their contrapositives.

When parents allow their children to spend a large amount of time watching television, those children see many more images of violence than do children who watch very little television. The more violent images a child sees, the more violent that child will become. The more violent a child is, the more likely the child is to commit crimes as an adult.

10. If the statements in the passage are true, which of the following must also be true?

A. With an increase in the number of acts of violence committed by children, one can expect to find a concurrent increase in the amount of television watched by children.

B. If parents did not allow their children to watch television, juvenile delinquency would be unlikely.

C. No child will develop an aversion to violence if he or she is permitted to watch television.

D. The more parents try to discourage their children from watching television, the more likely those children are to become criminals.

E. If a child sees more images of violence on television, the likelihood of that child committing crimes as an adult increases.

This argument lends itself to a quick paraphrase. First it states that when children watch a large amount of television, they see more images of violence. Therefore, it concludes that seeing images of violence leads to violence as a child and that violence as a child subsequently leads to an increased likelihood of crime as an adult. Following this causal chain through, more time watching TV increases the likelihood of crime as an adult.

(**E**) is the only choice that is consistent with this line of thinking.

As for the incorrect answers, (**A**) reverses the causal link in the stimulus. If a child watches more television, then that child commits a greater number of violent acts. That does not imply that if a child commits a greater number of violent acts, then that child watched more television. A child may be violent for other reasons.

**(B)** brings in the new term "juvenile delinquency" and is, therefore, outside the scope of the argument.

**(C)** uses extreme language and makes a claim that is not supported by the passage. To say that "no child" will develop an aversion to violence is the kind of extreme language that can quickly be eliminated on LSAT inference questions.

Lastly, **(D)** discusses parents "discouraging" their children from watching television. There is no mention of this in the original argument. It is outside the scope of the argument to bring in new ideas like parental discouragement, so no inferences can be made along these lines.

## Recap!

We have now covered the four main question types that appear on the Logical Reasoning section of the LSAT. In the following pages, we will quickly acquaint you with the remaining question types you can expect to see. Keep in mind that roughly two thirds of the questions you will see on these sections will be assumption, strengthen/weaken, logical flaw, and inference questions. The majority of your preparation time should be spent with those question types.

# EXPLAIN THE DISCREPANCY/PARADOX

Explain questions are a relatively uncommon Logical Reasoning question type. The stimulus to an explain question does not present an argument with evidence and a conclusion but rather describes a situation with two or more seemingly contradictory facts. Your job is to find the answer choice that explains away this seeming contradiction.

When a question asks you to . . .

- explain the discrepancy, situation, or result described;
- resolve the apparent paradox; or
- reconcile the contradiction

. . . you're being asked to explain how two or more seemingly contradictory facts can be true at the same time.

Before attempting to find an explanation, make sure you have a good grasp of the situation that needs explaining. Predicting what might explain the situation can help speed your scan through the answer choices.

Only one answer choice will address all of the facts in dispute. Wrong answer choices, on the other hand, usually touch upon only one of the facts in dispute, deepen the mystery, make an irrelevant comparison, or misrepresent the scope of the situation.

The number of applicants applying to top graduate programs has declined by more than 10 percent since the mid-1990s. Nonetheless, the number of students admitted to these same programs has not decreased appreciably, and the caliber of the students admitted, as measured by their undergraduate GPAs and standardized test scores, has actually improved markedly.

11. Which of the following, if true, best explains the seemingly contradictory trends described above?

A. The number of applicants applying to second- and third-tier graduate programs has also declined by more than 10 percent since the mid-1990s.

B. Many potential graduate school applicants are put off by the ever-increasing cost of a graduate education.

C. The higher premium offered to the graduates of top graduate programs has made the applicant pool increasingly competitive, discouraging those with lower GPAs or standardized test scores from applying.

D. Because of improved economic opportunities, particularly in Internet start-up companies and other high-tech industries, general interest in leaving the workforce to go to graduate school has waned in recent years.

E. The number of women applying to top graduate programs has increased since the mid-1990s, while at the same time the number of men applying to top graduate programs has declined.

The correct answer is (C). The passage sets up the following contradictory facts to be resolved:

- The number of applicants applying to top graduate programs has declined by more than 10 percent since the mid-1990s.

- The number of students admitted to these same programs has not decreased appreciably, and the caliber of the students admitted, as measured by their undergraduate GPAs and standardized test scores, has actually improved markedly.

(C) alone addresses both sides of the contradiction, explaining that these programs have become increasingly competitive due to the higher premium placed on getting a grad degree from these institutions and that this in turn has discouraged those with lower GPAs and test scores from even bothering to apply.

(A) is outside the scope of the situation to be addressed. We are not interested in trends in graduate programs other than the top ones.

(B) addresses only one side of the contradiction. The ever-increasing cost of grad school may help explain why the number of applicants to top schools has gone down, but it does nothing to address why the caliber of those applying has nonetheless improved.

(D) likewise only addresses the first side of the contradiction. Nowhere does it explain why the caliber of the remaining applicants has improved.

Finally, (E) introduces an irrelevant comparison. The fact that more women and fewer men are applying to top graduate programs does nothing to address either side of the contradiction.

# METHOD OF ARGUMENT

Method of argument questions are a relatively uncommon Logical Reasoning question type. These questions are more concerned with what the author is doing or how the author gets the point across than with the nuts and bolts of the argument itself.

When a question asks you to what a disputant in a dialogue or the author of an argument is doing in an argument, this is an MOA (method of argument) question.

---

**STRATEGY TIP**

In MOA questions, leave out your critical judgment. Analyze the mechanics, not the merits, of the argument. If the method of argument doesn't jump out at you, then work backward from the answer choices. The correct answer has to contain each element of an argument to be correct. Never bend over backward to accept an answer choice.

---

*Theresa:* It is ridiculous to regard all emotional disorders as diseases and pretend that people have no control over them. Even calling something like obsessive gambling an "emotional disorder" is misguided; such behavioral problems should be recognized as character flaws, because people are responsible for their own actions.

*Barbara:* But if people view behavioral problems like obsessive gambling or compulsive eating as rooted in their own characters, they will fall into a cycle of self-blame and helplessness and fail to seek out professional treatment that could help them.

12. In her disagreement with Theresa, Barbara does which one of the following?

A. Attempts to disprove Theresa's conclusion by introducing new evidence

B. Shows that Theresa's use of the term *emotional disorder* is ambiguous

C. Accepts Theresa's conclusion but disputes the reasoning behind that conclusion

D. Argues that the problem Theresa wishes to address is not as serious as she believes

E. Does not directly dispute Theresa's conclusion but argues that her suggestion would have undesirable consequences

Only **(E)** completely captures Barbara's method of argument. Keep in mind that by reading the question stem first on questions such as this one, you save yourself valuable time by focusing your attack on the stimulus. Notice that Barbara does not question Theresa's conclusion that it is ridiculous to regard all emotional disorders as diseases and pretend that people have no control over them. Instead, she contends that if people accepted Theresa's suggestion, they would fail to seek out the professional treatment that could help them.

**(A)** misses the point by claiming that Barbara is attempting to disprove Theresa's argument.

**(B)** is incorrect. Barbara does not even mention the term *emotional disorder* in her rebuttal.

**(C)** misses the point. Barbara focuses less on Theresa's reasoning than on the consequences of her argument.

**(D)** is contrary to what Barbara is saying. If anything, Barbara feels that the problems Theresa is discussing are more serious than Theresa believes.

Only **(E)** accurately captures the structure of Barbara's objection to Theresa's argument.

We will continue to explore the structure, rather than the content, of arguments with the final question type we will look at—parallel reasoning.

# PARALLEL REASONING

Parallel reasoning questions are a relatively uncommon Logical Reasoning question type. You can expect a total of four questions of this type, two per LR section. Much like method of argument questions, these questions are more concerned with the structure, as opposed to the content, of arguments.

For example, look at the following stimulus:

> All fraternity members misbehave at parties. Since Ed isn't in a fraternity, he must never misbehave at parties.
>
> Which one of the following most closely parallels the flawed reasoning in the argument above?

When faced with a question like this, attack the original argument and attempt to isolate its structure irrespective of its content.

---

**STRATEGY TIP**

Parallel reasoning questions tend to be quite time consuming. Consequently, we recommend that you skip these questions and handle them only after you have looked at all of the other questions within a section. When short on time, a quick scan of the stimulus and answer choices allows you to rule out several answer choices and make a good guess.

---

On parallel reasoning questions, it is frequently helpful to rewrite the argument using a more algebraic representation. Although the order in which the information is presented may change, the correct answer will always have every element you see in the original argument. Begin by matching up conclusion to conclusion when possible.

Let's apply this tip to the argument we looked at previously, working through the argument one piece at a time:

"All fraternity members misbehave at parties" becomes *All A's do B*.

"Since Ed isn't in a fraternity" becomes *Ed is not an A*.

"He must never misbehave at parties" becomes *Ed does not do B*.

So our rephrase of the argument is:

*All A's do B.*
*Ed is not an A.*
*Therefore, Ed does not do B.*

The next step is to go through each choice and look for the answer that corresponds to the structure above. Remember that the order of the elements might change, but each piece of the structure outlined above must be contained in the correct answer choice.

Let's look at this argument as it might appear on the LSAT.

All fraternity members misbehave at parties. Since Ed isn't in a fraternity, he must never misbehave at parties.

13. Which one of the following most closely parallels the reasoning in this argument?

   A. All Westerns are dull. Since *The Longest Day* isn't dull, it must not be a Western.

   B. Most taxi dispatchers work long shifts. Since Leo isn't a taxi dispatcher, he usually works an eight-hour day.

   C. Fred must have a good disposition, because he doesn't have a stressful job. People with stressful jobs always have a terrible disposition.

   D. Well-traveled people talk a lot about where they've been. Since Todd hasn't traveled, he must be a very interesting conversationalist.

   E. All automobiles are parked on the right-hand side of the street on Sunday mornings. That car is parked on the left, so it must not be mine.

We are looking for a structure similar to the following:

*All A's do B.*
*X is not an A.*
*Therefore, X does not do B.*

Keep in mind that on these time-consuming problems, a quick scan of the answer choices can help tremendously. Notice that the argument above uses the term *all*. Scanning the answer choices, you can quickly eliminate **(B)** for its use of *most* instead of *all*.

**(A)** is tempting because it is arranged very similarly to the stimulus. "All Westerns are dull" is roughly equivalent to *All A's do B,* but the second line "Since *The Longest Day* isn't dull" translates to *X is not B* as opposed to *X is not A.* Therefore, you can eliminate **(A)**.

**(B)** uses *most* instead of *all*, so you can eliminate it.

**(C)** takes some time to sort out. The first half of the first sentence looks like the conclusion of our stimulus. "Fred must have a good disposition" corresponds to *Therefore X does not do B* (where B is having a bad disposition). The second half of the first sentence, "because he doesn't have a stressful job" corresponds to *X is not A*. Finally, the last sentence, "people with stressful jobs always have a terrible disposition," corresponds to *All A's do B*. In all, the argument is parallel to the stimulus, and **(C)** is the correct answer.

**(D)** and **(E)** can be eliminated because each introduces an extra concept to the argument. **(D)** adds the idea of "a very interesting conversationalist," and **(E)** says that "the car must not be mine." The correct answer always has a one-to-one correspondence of elements to the elements in the stimulus.

In all, these questions can take some time and require some careful, methodical thought. Unless you are very comfortable and quick with this question type, skip them until the end of your exam.

# CONCLUSION

There are several key ideas to keep in mind when handling a Logical Reasoning section on the LSAT.

## TIME MANAGEMENT

Time management is essential to mastering the Logical Reasoning sections of the LSAT. You have 35 minutes to answer roughly 25 questions. That is not a lot of time. On average, each Logical Reasoning question should take you roughly 1 minute and 15 seconds. When working through practice sets, keep this time frame in mind. Understand which questions you can handle in less than a minute and which question types will take two minutes and longer. Use this to develop your game plan heading into your test.

## LSAT Mindset

Plan on making at least two passes through a Logical Reasoning section. During the first pass, handle the questions you feel most confident and efficient answering. Each subsequent pass through a section can address questions you find tougher or more time consuming. When handling an LR section, keep these three ideas in mind:

- Answer questions *if* you want to (by guessing on the most difficult questions rather than wasting time on them).

- Answer questions *when* you want to (by skipping parallel reasoning and other tricky or time-consuming questions until later in the test). However, if you don't get to every question in the section, remember always to guess and fill in an answer for every question in the section!

- Answering questions *how* you want to (by using our shortcuts and strategies to get points quickly and confidently, even if those methods aren't exactly what the test makers had in mind).

The key is to feel in control of your test and to play to your strengths. A big part of this involves knowing what your strengths in logical reasoning are.

As we have reviewed in this chapter, the two LSAT Logical Reasoning sections account for roughly one half of your LSAT score. We have explored in depth assumption, strengthen/weaken, and faulty logic questions, which require you to attack a stimulus systematically and identify its evidence, conclusion, and assumptions. Of the remaining question types, inferences are the most common; these test your ability to make logical deductions based on the information you are given in a stimulus. In addition to inference questions, we also looked at several other common question types that appear on the LSAT. These question types tend to focus more on the structure of an argument than its content.

Here's a recap of our method for attacking Logic Reasoning questions systematically.

**Step 1: Read the question stem first.** When you first encounter a Logical Reasoning question, decide quickly whether to do it now or later. Read the question stem first to see if it is a question type you feel comfortable tackling at that time. Play to your own strengths. Some questions take a good deal of time to answer, while others can be handled within a minute or so. Understanding yourself as a test taker and playing to your strengths is the key to significant score improvements on the LSAT.

**Step 2: Use the information in the question stem to focus your attack on the stimulus.** Different question types require slightly different approaches. Quite a few questions require you to look for an argument's key assumptions. Others will require you to make inferences based on the information you have been given. Still others will ask you to understand the structure, or method, to an argument. Regardless, the question stem will give you invaluable clues that will focus your attack on the stimulus.

**Step 3: Attack the stimulus.** On assumption, strengthen/weaken, and flaw questions, isolate the conclusion (the author's main point) and the evidence (the support the author provides for that point). Identify any assumptions (unstated yet necessary premises) that fill in gaps between the evidence and conclusion. On inference questions, a paraphrase of the argument is most helpful. For method of argument or parallel reasoning questions, a sense of the overall structure of the argument is what you are reading for.

**Step 4: Whenever possible, predict the answer before you examine the answer choices.** This saves you time and prevents you from falling prey to trap answer choices. However, for inference and parallel reasoning questions, for instance, coming up with a prediction might not be so easy. In these cases, proceed directly to the answer choices.

**Step 5: Attack the answer choices** and choose the one that comes closest to your prediction. A quick scan of the answer choices for a match of your prediction, instead of reading through and evaluating each choice, can save valuable time. Avoid choices that use extreme language or are outside the scope of the argument. When stuck, evaluate choices, eliminate obviously incorrect answers, take a guess, and move on.

## FINAL THOUGHTS

### Make the Most of Your Prep Time
If you are reading this book, then time is of the essence, and your preparation should reflect that. Although we have covered quite a few different question types, where you focus your efforts will have a profound influence on your ability to improve your performance.

## Focus on the High-Yield Concepts and Question Types

Assumption, strengthen/weaken, faulty logic, and inference questions account for roughly two thirds of the Logical Reasoning questions you will see on the LSAT. Understanding the structure of arguments, assumptions, typical flaws, and inferences will give you the strong foundation you need to ace the Logical Reasoning sections of the LSAT. Only after you have mastered these fundamental concepts and question types should you look at other types of LR questions.

## Play to Your Strengths

As you prepare for the LSAT, pay close attention to two things: **performance** and **timing**. Knowing which question types you handle best and which question types you handle most quickly will help set up your LR game plan come Test Day.

Once the test begins, seek out the types of questions you have mastered and answer them first. Remember, you will earn the lion's share of your points from the questions you feel most comfortable with. Save the questions that take the most time and give you the most trouble for last. Trust your instincts and learn when to take guesses on the LR questions that give you the most trouble.

This knowledge comes from practice, so begin by taking the post-test that follows. We've also included exhaustive explanations to the post-test questions, which underscore the strategies you've learned in this chapter.

Enjoy law school and . . . best of luck on Test Day!

## PRACTICE SET

Advertisement: Are you having trouble returning your opponents' power serves? The new Spring-Strung rackets are designed to improve your tennis game overnight without lessons. Even rank amateurs can effortlessly increase the speed and force of their volleys by 25 percent. You too can achieve the power of a professional player with the Spring-Strung racket.

1.  Someone who accepted the reasoning in this advertisement would be making which one of the following assumptions?

    A.  Without quality equipment, a tennis player cannot improve his game.

    B.  The Spring-Strung racket will improve an amateur's game more than it will improve a professional's game.

    C.  The quality of a person's tennis game is largely determined by the speed and force of his volley.

    D.  The Spring-Strung racket is superior to any other racket currently on the market.

    E.  Lessons are not as effective at improving the speed and force of a player's volley as is the use of quality equipment.


All human beings are either optimists or pessimists. Joey is not a pessimist. Therefore, Joey is an optimist.

2.  Which one of the following is assumed by the argument above?

    A.  Joey is a human being.

    B.  Optimists are never pessimistic about anything.

    C.  Joey does not believe himself to be a pessimist.

    D.  Joey does not allow disappointments to upset him.

    E.  More people are optimists than are pessimists.

The board of directors of the Lejon Etymological Museum imposed a 50-cent admission charge to reduce the museum's deficit. Attendance remained stable and there was no protest from the public, so six months later, the museum announced that the admission price would go up to $1.50.

3. It can be inferred that, in increasing the admission charge to $1.50, the board of directors assumed that

   A. people did not protest the initial charge because they felt it was necessary to keep the museum in operation.

   B. because people did not protest the initial charge, they will also accept the raised price.

   C. because $1.50 is three times the original charge, it is probable that attendance will drop as the public protests the increase.

   D. the increased revenue from admissions will enable the museum to expand its operations.

   E. tripling the admission cost every six months will not cause a drop in attendance.

Every week, 40,000 Americans come home to an unexpectedly open front door and a ransacked home. Protect yourself against this potential tragedy: install a Safe-T lock. Safe-T's five-layered protective steel plate and 60 billion computer-controlled combinations make it one of the finest locks money can buy. We've sold 12 million Safe-T locks in the past ten years and haven't received a single report of one of them being picked.

4. The claim in this advertisement would be most seriously undermined if it were true that

   A. many homes that are broken into are not actually burglarized.

   B. Safe-T's major competitor has received no reports of its own locks being picked.

   C. most customers install Safe-T locks only to supplement other locks.

   D. most people report thefts and picked locks only to their local police precinct.

   E. the majority of thieves enter homes through a back or side door.

Nigel must be a judge because he is wearing a black robe and judges always wear black robes.

5.  Which one of the following statements could NOT be used to challenge the validity of the argument above?

    A.  Clergymen often wear black robes.

    B.  College professors sometimes wear black robes.

    C.  Nigel doesn't always wear a black robe.

    D.  There are many other criteria more significant than wardrobe that determines whether or not one is a judge.

    E.  Funeral directors always wear black.

The industrialized nations should not feed the people of developing countries because doing so will simply enable them to continue overpopulating. Then we will have to provide even more assistance, and eventually, more will suffer because we won't be able to feed them at all.

6.  Which one of the following statements, if true, would seriously weaken the author's argument?

    A.  Recent developments in synthetic agriculture provide convincing evidence that food production can increase indefinitely at a rate higher than that of world population growth.

    B.  A population study just released indicates that the population of one small developing country in West Africa has decreased by 10 percent in the last decade.

    C.  A Red Cross spokesperson announced last month that unless industrialized nations immediately increase their aid to developing countries, record numbers of children and the elderly will die of starvation.

    D.  At a recent conference of leaders of industrialized nations, it was concluded that it is immoral to do nothing to prevent starvation.

    E.  Religious leaders in developing countries have recently issued a ban on population control measures proposed by industrialized nations.

A criminal was sentenced to several years in federal prison for theft. During that time, he wrote a novel, which somehow managed to find its way into the hands of the most renowned literary figures in the country. Overwhelmed by the novel's brilliant prose, these writers immediately went to the federal government and argued for the prisoner's release on the grounds that someone with so much talent obviously did not belong in prison. The prisoner later went on to receive the highest literary award his country had to offer.

7. The writers' argument assumes which one of the following?

   A. Literary talent can in some way compensate for criminal tendencies.

   B. The prisoner had been reformed during the time he had spent in jail.

   C. The prisoner's novel would be well received by readers outside of the literary community.

   D. The criminal's experiences in jail provided interesting subject matter for his novel.

   E. If the prisoner had remained in jail, he would eventually have lost his ability to write.

The state lawmakers' critics warned that if the lawmakers carried out their plan to overturn the existing legislation requiring all mental health personnel to report patients' murder threats to the potential victims, there would be an increase in the number of homicides in the state. Because the legislation has just been overturned, the state should prepare itself for an increase in the murder rate.

8. Which one of the following, if true, would most strengthen this argument?

   A. The vast majority of people who make murder threats do not intend to carry them out.

   B. During the first year the legislation was enacted, violent crime fell by nearly 5 percent.

   C. Most violent patients of mental health personnel are confined to high-security psychiatric institutions.

D. Many patients of mental health professionals make numerous threats against others, often against individuals personally unknown to them.

E. A positive correlation between warning a potential murder victim and the later prevention of the threatened murder has been shown to exist.

State revenues from the corporate income tax are seriously threatened by the new trend toward decentralization of corporate headquarters. Many of the companies leaving the city, with its extensive public transportation system, are finding it necessary to import costly executive helicopters to transport personnel to and from isolated locations in the suburbs. Because money spent on these helicopters is deductible from gross corporate income as an expense of doing business, such companies will thus pay lower taxes to the state. We must apply appropriate economic sanctions to avoid the loss of these much-needed tax revenues.

9. Which one of the following identifies the main weakness in the reasoning behind the argument?

A. The writer fails to suggest alternative modes of transportation less costly than helicopters.

B. The writer fails to demonstrate that higher personnel transport costs are not offset by other economies at the new corporate headquarters.

C. The writer fails to consider the increased taxes paid by the helicopter manufacturers as a result of booming business.

D. The writer fails to consider the higher productivity achieved through rapid helicopter travel.

E. The writer fails to specify other economic difficulties caused by the corporations' flight from the city.

The form of the Petrarchan sonnet fosters a more exquisite literary experience than does the form of the detective novel. We can be assured of this truth by the fact that the best critics, those with delicate sensibilities, inevitably prefer the Petrarchan sonnet to the detective novel. And we know these critics to be superior by their preference for the Petrarchan sonnet.

10. A proper critique of the logic expressed in this argument would most likely point out that the author

A. fails to cite specific critical authorities.

B. assumes the point he wishes to establish.

C. generalizes from a specific example to a general rule.

D. does not provide evidence in support of his conclusion.

E. fails to provide exceptions to the classification he outlines.

People who play chess as a hobby should not be discouraged by the recent record-breaking season of Anatoly Krupnik, the great Russian master. By far the most important factor in determining the quality of one's game is the amount of time one puts into practicing the basics. Even Anatoly Krupnik was once an uninitiated beginner.

11. Which one of the following best expresses the author's main point?

A. Even chess masters begin by playing the game as a hobby.

B. Although time and effort spent mastering the fundamentals is of some importance, it will not train one to play as well as Anatoly Krupnik.

C. If one puts in enough time practicing the basics of chess, one will eventually play the game as well as Anatoly Krupnik.

D. Regardless of how much time and effort one has put into practicing the game of chess, luck is the most important factor in determining one's eventual success.

E. Practicing the basics of chess is the best way to become a quality chess player.

There can be little doubt that electoral suffrage is power. Of course, power must be wielded with reason, and in our present society, there appears to be no way to achieve this except by giving a vote to everyone. But when all have votes, it will be both just in principle and necessary in fact that some mode be adopted for giving greater weight to the suffrage of the more educated voter, some means by which the one who is more capable and competent in the general affairs of life and who possesses more of the knowledge applicable to the management of the affairs of the community could be singled out and allowed a superiority of influence proportional to his higher qualifications.

12. The author's primary purpose is to argue that

    A. not everyone should be allowed to vote.

    B. not all men are equal.

    C. a dictatorship is preferable to a democracy.

    D. the more knowledgeable members of society should have more power at the voting booth.

    E. some kind of test to evaluate civic virtue should be made a prerequisite to granting a citizen the right to vote.

If I go to class tomorrow without having done the reading, my professor will call on me and be angry that I am not prepared. But if I stay up all night, which is what I would have to do to catch up on the reading, he will be angry because I will be too tired to stay awake in class.

13. This argument is constructed to lead to which one of the following conclusions?

    A. If I go to class tomorrow, my professor will be angry at me.

    B. If I stay home tomorrow to catch up on the reading, my professor will be angry that I skipped class.

    C. It would be better for me to skip class tomorrow than to stay up late reading.

    D. My professor will be angry.

    E. If my professor is angry at me, it is because I fell behind on the reading.

One of the most striking facets of the history of jazz in America is the relationship between improvisation and band arrangement. Early New Orleans jazz was almost totally improvised, but by the time of Chicago jazz in the '30s, only one soloist at a time had any real freedom. In the '40s, the band arrangers reigned supreme, as the big bands relied on their intricate arrangements, even for soloists. Then the pendulum swung back with bebop, and improvisation returned to the fore. In the '70s and '80s, jazz pieces once again came increasingly to be written down, and performers again found themselves in a period of complicated but confining arrangements.

14. Which one of the following is probably the conclusion toward which the author is moving?

    A. Apparently, then, the history of jazz does not conform to any coherent progression of styles.

    B. These written arrangements of jazz therefore result in an unfortunate lack of freedom for the soloists.

    C. Thus, the history of jazz seems to take the shape of a cyclical movement from improvisation to arrangement and back again.

    D. It would seem, then, that jazz has been fraught with inconsistencies such as these throughout its history.

    E. The band and the soloist, then, continue to vie for the limelight in the history of jazz.

15. The author would probably argue that the next style in jazz history will be characterized by

    A. extensive improvisation.

    B. intricate big band arrangements.

    C. freedom for one soloist at a time.

    D. written scores for soloists only.

    E. a return to New Orleans jazz.

The only vehicles that have come across the bridge since dusk have been tanks. All of the tanks that came across the bridge since dusk were light tanks. Thus, all of the vehicles that have come across the bridge since dusk have been light.

16. Which one of the following exhibits faulty reasoning most similar to the faulty reasoning exhibited in the passage?

   A. The only flowers in the garden are roses, and all of the roses in the garden are red. Therefore, all of the flowers in the garden are red flowers.

   B. All of the bears in the zoo are carnivores. All of the bears in the zoo are also large. Thus, all carnivores are large.

   C. The only objects on the showroom floor are kitchen appliances. All of the kitchen appliances on the showroom floor come with two-year warranties. Therefore, all of the objects on the showroom floor come with two-year warranties.

   D. All of the objects that spilled out upon the counter were rocks from Professor Wainright's collection. Professor Wainright's collection is exclusively made up of soft rocks. Thus, all of the objects that spilled out upon the counter were soft.

   E. All of the paintings hanging in the gallery are oil paintings. The only paintings in the gallery are still-lifes and portraits. Therefore, all of the portraits hanging in the gallery are oil paintings.

There is no doubt that situation comedies are escapist nonsense. We can conclude, therefore, that television is detrimental to the education of children.

17. This argument is most like which one of the following?

   A. Music soothes the savage breast; therefore, the arts are beneficial to society's mental health.

   B. My brother is an actor; therefore, he is egotistical and does not respond well to others.

   C. Drugs are bad for people; therefore, taking aspirin is not a wise practice for invalids.

   D. Terrorism is on the rise; therefore, people are not very concerned about law and order anymore.

   E. Scavengers are highly adaptable; therefore, rats are among the most versatile of animals.

Olympic swimmers have been shown to have between 3 and 10 percent body fat. If we could all decrease our body fat to that level, we would all swim better.

18. Which one of the following most accurately characterizes the method of reasoning used in this statement?

   A. It bases a conclusion on evidence about the argument's source.

   B. It illustrates the absurdity of the argument by reaching an illogical conclusion.

   C. It uses flawed evidence to support its conclusion.

   D. It assumes what it seeks to establish.

   E. It assumes a causal relationship is responsible for a correlation.

The government should repeal the national speed limit, which was originally enacted as a conservation measure in response to the fuel shortages of the 1970s. With the discovery of new domestic oil reserves and the availability of new foreign suppliers, the nation is no longer faced with a shortage of fuel needed to run automobiles.

19. Which one of the following principles, if established, most strongly supports the recommendation to repeal the national speed limit?

    A. A statute should be repealed unless it can be demonstrated that it can still accomplish the goal for which it was originally designed.

    B. When a statute ceases to serve a useful purpose, the statute should be repealed.

    C. Wherever possible, statutes should be modified to reflect changing national consensus.

    D. An effort should be made to explain the reasons for a statute's enactment to all those who are affected by the statute.

    E. When the original situation that prompted the enactment of a statute no longer exists, the statute should be repealed.

*Madeleine:* It is unwise as well as immoral for people living in one section of the country to use their greater political power to pass laws that will result in the environmental degradation of another section of the country. Because the environment of the whole country is one interconnected system, any environmental degradation that occurs in one section will inevitably result in similar damage in every other section of the country.

*Grant:* The different sections of the country are more or less closed environmental systems, so what happens in one section is unlikely to have any effect on any other section. It is unwise for people living in one section of the country to cause the environmental degradation of another section of the country because it would lead to widespread resentment among the people living in the affected section.

20. Based on their stated positions, Madeleine and Grant are committed to disagreeing about which one of the following?

    A. Whether there is any moral obligation to preserve the environment for future generations

    B. Whether any one section of the country has the political power to pass laws that affect the environment of another section of the country

    C. Whether an action causing environmental degradation in one section of the country will inevitably have a negative effect on the environment of another section of the country

    D. Whether people in any section of the country are likely to impose laws that will result in the environmental degradation of another section of the country

    E. Whether it is good policy for people in one section of the country to attempt to preserve the environmental health of any other section of the country

# ANSWERS AND EXPLANATIONS

## ANSWER KEY

| | | | |
|---|---|---|---|
| 1. C | 6. A | 11. E | 16. D |
| 2. A | 7. A | 12. D | 17. A |
| 3. B | 8. E | 13. A | 18. E |
| 4. D | 9. B | 14. C | 19. E |
| 5. D | 10. B | 15. A | 20. C |

**1. (C)**

This ad presents three claims: that Spring-Strung rackets improve your game overnight, that amateurs effortlessly increase the speed and force of their volleys by 25 percent with Spring-Strung rackets, and that you can achieve the power of a pro with a Spring-Strung racket. The only evidence that's cited to explain how this racket improves your game is in the third sentence of the ad: amateurs can increase the speed and force of their volleys. Therefore, **(C)** must be assumed. If it is not assumed, then there is no reason to think that this racket will improve one's game.

**(A)** is wrong because it is not assumed that quality equipment is necessary to improve a player's game but rather that this equipment is sufficient to do so.

As for **(B)**, the ad is aimed at the amateur, but for all you know, this racket does as much for a pro's game as for that of an amateur. Thus, **(B)** is not assumed.

**(D)** is outside the scope, as this racket is never compared to any other rackets on the market.

As for **(E)**, the ad never compares the effectiveness of this racket to that of lessons; for all you know, lessons may be more effective, even if they take longer and require more work.

## 2. (A)

The argument consists of two premises and a conclusion. All human beings are either optimists or pessimists. So if someone is human, then he or she is either an optimist or a pessimist. Next, you're told that Joey is not a pessimist. You do not know whether or not Joey is human. Only if Joey is human can the information given in the first premise apply to him. The conclusion is that Joey must be an optimist, so this choice, that Joey is human, is being assumed. When this is assumed, the argument becomes perfectly valid.

**(B)** is not assumed because it's not made clear that the author considers optimists to be people who are always without a trace of pessimism. The author could be referring to people who are optimistic in general.

**(C)** isn't assumed because the argument is concerned with what humans are (i.e., optimists or pessimists), not with what they think they are.

**(D)** is similar to **(B)**. You don't know if the author considers optimists to be people who don't allow disappointments to upset them; again, they could simply be people who are generally optimistic.

**(E)** is wrong because nowhere is the number of optimists mentioned, let alone compared to the number of pessimists.

## 3. (B)

On the basis of the evidence that there was no protest to a 50-cent museum admission charge, the board concluded that it could safely raise the price to $1.50. The unstated assumption is that because the public tolerated the 50-cent charge, it will also tolerate the higher charge. **(B)** is precisely what the board did assume, and it is all it assumed. Otherwise, it would not have raised the price, using the acceptance of the earlier price rise as evidence.

**(A)** is wrong because there's nothing in the passage to make you think the board paid any attention to why the 50-cent admission charge was not protested.

**(C)** is not assumed. People may protest the price hike, but this is what the board hopes will not happen and so is not what the board assumed when it raised the admission charge to $1.50.

**(D)** is outside the scope. The argument never mentions what the board plans to do with the increased revenues.

**(E)** is rather silly. Future admission increases are beyond the scope, and it would be ludicrous for the board to assume that it can triple the admission every six months without causing attendance to drop.

### 4. (D)

Advertisements can be arguments, too. The conclusion here is that the Safe-T lock's features make it "one of the finest locks money can buy." This conclusion is supported by some evidence: 1) a description of the lock and 2) the fact that the manufacturer has not received a single report of a picked Safe-T lock in the past decade. Of course, for this evidence to support this conclusion, one assumption the author must be making is that people would report any picked locks to the manufacturer. If this is not true, any information regarding such reporting is not an accurate reflection of how many customers have their locks picked. **(D)**, by undermining this essential assumption, undermines the argument.

**(A)** is irrelevant, because the evidence is not about the number of actual burglaries reported to the manufacturers but rather about the number of picked locks, burglary or no burglary.

**(B)** doesn't weaken the claim because Safe-T never said it was the finest lock around, just that it was one of the finest locks around.

**(C)** seems to suggest that Safe-T's spotless performance record may be due to the presence of other locks on the same doors, but again, the evidence is just about Safe-T locks and whether they alone were picked, regardless of how many other locks may have been on the doors.

**(E)** has no effect on the argument until we know whether or not those back and side doors were protected by Safe-T locks.

### 5. (D)

You're given the evidence that all judges wear black robes and that Nigel is wearing a black robe. The conclusion is that Nigel must be a judge. The most glaring assumption is that only judges wear black robes. The only statement that fails to weaken this argument is **(E)**, which is irrelevant. The argument assumes that only judges wear black robes; **(E)**'s assertion that funeral directors wear black doesn't contradict this.

(A) and (B) weaken the argument by doing what (E) failed to do: point out that people besides judges wear black robes.

(C) weakens the argument by pointing out that Nigel, unlike judges according to the stimulus, doesn't always wear a black robe.

(D) directly attacks the reasoning by pointing out that one must consider other criteria more important than wardrobe when deciding if someone is a judge.

### 6. (A)

(A) weakens the argument by attacking one of the author's assumptions—that an industrialized country's ability to produce food has a ceiling, or an upper limit. (Another assumption is that overpopulation will, indeed, result.) It also states that we will be able to feed all the people that will be born if we go ahead and feed starving people now, and if that's true, the argument falls apart.

(B) states that the population of one particular developing country has decreased, but that does not attack the assumption that feeding starving people in developing countries will result in overpopulation. Maybe the country's population declined because of starvation.

(C) says that if we don't feed starving people, many of them will die. Because the author has already asserted that if we do feed these people now, even more of them will starve in the future, this choice is consistent with the argument.

As for (D), the author would simply respond that doing nothing about starvation now is doing something about future starvation; namely, it's preventing famine among future generations.

(E) actually strengthens the argument. The fact that birth control is banned in developing countries supports the claim that overpopulation will continue to be a problem.

### 7. (A)

Because the writers argued that the prisoner should be released (their conclusion) because someone so talented did not belong in prison (their evidence), they must assume (A). Use the denial test to make sure that this choice is correct: if the writers assumed literary talent did not compensate somewhat for criminal tendencies, they'd have no reason to argue for releasing the prisoner.

The other four choices are all outside the scope. Nothing in the argument addresses the issue of reform, **(B)**; the novel's reception, **(C)**; its subject matter, **(D)**; or whether or not the prisoner would lose his ability to write if he stayed in jail, **(E)**. Their argument is based on his talent as a writer, pure and simple.

### 8. (E)

The critics warned that if the existing law were repealed, and mental health personnel no longer warned potential victims of the murder threats made by their patients, the state would see an increase in the number of murders. The evidence ends with the statement that the law has just been repealed. The conclusion expressed is that the state will very likely see an increase in the murder rate. To pick the statement that most strengthens this argument, you want the choice that makes it more likely that overturning the established law will result in a higher incidence of murders. You want a choice that screams, "Bring back the law!" **(E)** fits the bill. If there's a positive correlation between warning a potential murder victim and saving that potential victim's life, then the law was doing good work, and with its repeal, you can expect a higher murder rate.

**(A)** seems to be saying that a murder threat is nothing to get too alarmed about. **(A)**, therefore, doesn't strengthen the argument, and it doesn't make it more likely that there will soon be an increase in the number of murders.

**(B)** wants you to think that with the repeal of the law, the murder rate will go up 5 percent. However, it refers to all violent crime, not just murders, so we have no way of knowing whether the law had any effect on the incidence of murders in the state.

**(C)** implies that dangerous patients are safely isolated in high-security institutions. This would tend to weaken the argument, showing that these people are unlikely to kill anyone, regardless of the warning.

Finally, **(D)** just points to the number of threats made by mental health patients, while leaving open the question of whether these threats are later carried out. If the threats are not carried out, then there is little to worry about, even though the law has been repealed.

## 9. (B)

The author recommends a course of action, the application of economic sanctions, because the relocation of companies from city to isolated suburbs has decreased the contribution made to state revenues by the corporate income tax. How, specifically? The new locations require expensive helicopter transportation for personnel; this expense is deductible from corporate tax payments. The assumption here is that the corporate moves have not also had the contrary effect upon a company's total deductible business expenses. In other words, as suggested in **(B)**, the paragraph takes for granted that "other economies" have not accompanied the move to the suburban locations, thus offsetting the effect of the increased transportation costs and sustaining or possibly raising the total amounts paid in corporate income taxes. (What if the rent is lower because the office is not in a city but a suburb, or what if some employees receive lower compensation because they live in the suburbs and have less far to travel? Either or both of these possibilities could reduce the amount deductible by the company.)

**(A)** misses the point on several fronts. First, the author does refer to the helicopters as "necessary," thus making any alternative unsatisfactory. More importantly, nothing in the author's statement requires her to suggest alternatives to the helicopter for the argument to be complete. The author thinks that companies that leave the city should be sanctioned for the state to avoid losing tax revenues it is entitled to. How this tax revenue gets there (through sanctions, through lower-costing transportation, or because a company is still located in the city) is not essential to the argument. The author's argument involves a growing category of companies *supposedly* paying less of one kind of tax than they should. As noted earlier, the real issue here is whether these companies are actually deducting a larger total amount from this tax bill than before the move.

**(C)** is based on at least two unwarranted assumptions: that (1) the helicopters are manufactured in the state whose finances are being discussed and (2) even in that event, the taxes generated would be at least as great as the amount lost from the taxes of the companies using the helicopters. There is no justification for assuming either of these to be the case. In fact, the helicopters are described as "imported," indicating that they were manufactured elsewhere.

In **(D)**, there is a similar reliance upon unjustified assumptions. While it is possible that helicopter travel in the suburbs might have the effect of increasing productivity above levels in the city (with its mass transit), it is not very likely, the frequency of subway delays notwithstanding. Nor do you know that this supposed rise in taxes would be great enough to offset the loss, that the author of the passage now deplores.

As for **(E)**, the author is not required to demonstrate any difficulties other than that mentioned in the passage. As long as helicopter use reduces tax income, the argument stands.

### 10. (B)

The author concludes that a more exquisite literary experience is to be had from a Petrarchan sonnet than from a detective novel. The evidence used to support this claim is that the best critics agree with it; the "best critics" are defined as those who prefer the Petrarchan sonnet to the detective novel. Thus, the conclusion (the superiority of the sonnets) is presupposed in the evidence (in the identification of who are the best critics). This is circular reasoning. For this argument to work, some other criterion would be needed to determine the qualifications of the critics. As it now stands, it is logically flawed, and this flaw is described by **(B)**. The author assumes the point he wishes to argue.

**(A)** does a little damage, as the author has never named one of the critical authorities. Yet that's not the main flaw here; the main flaw is the criterion used in deciding who the best authorities are.

**(C)** is incorrect for the simple reason that no specific example is given.

**(D)** is incorrect because the author does provide evidence, the best critics' opinions; the problem resides in the fact that the evidence is inappropriate.

**(E)** is incorrect because the author need not provide exceptions; he may not believe that there are any exceptions.

## 11. (E)

The conclusion the author makes is that chess hobbyists should not be discouraged by the great success of a Russian master. The evidence is that even this man was once an uninitiated beginner and that time spent practicing the basics is the most important factor in improving one's game. Therefore, the point is that knowing and practicing the basics is what made this master's game superb and such practice can make your game superb, relatively speaking. The author, then, is making the point in **(E)**, that practicing the basics will improve your chess game.

**(A)** is out because while the great masters had to start as beginners, you cannot be sure that they began playing chess as a hobby. Perhaps they considered it as serious training for a later occupation.

**(B)** says that no matter how much you practice, you will never be as good as Krupnik, the master; however, there is no hint of that pessimism in the argument.

**(C)** reverses **(B)** and implies that enough practice guarantees skills as good as those of Krupnik. Again, no such claim is made.

**(D)** completely contradicts the author's point. The author considers practice the most important factor, not luck.

## 12. (D)

The author argues that because people are unequal in terms of their education and capability, not all votes should be weighed equally. Those who are most knowledgeable should be entrusted with greater decision-making power. Thus, this choice provides the author's primary purpose.

**(A)** and **(E)** are incorrect because the author states that everyone in this society should be given a vote to ensure that power is wielded with reason. Because both these answer choices suggest that not everyone should be allowed to vote, they contradict the author.

**(B)** is an assumption of the argument rather than something the author tries to prove. By advocating a weighted voting system on the basis of how "capable" and "competent" an individual is, the author assumes that these people are not equal.

The author doesn't discuss the merits of dictatorship, **(C)**, so you cannot be certain what she thinks about it.

## 13. (A)

The student can either go to class unprepared, in which case her professor will be angry, or she can stay up all night reading, in which case she'll fall asleep in class, thereby incurring her professor's wrath. This is a no-win situation: if she goes to class tomorrow, whether or not she's done the reading, her professor will be angry at her, which is **(A)**.

You were never told what would happen if the student doesn't go to class tomorrow, so **(B)** is out.

For the same reason, you cannot conclude **(C)**—you don't know the consequences of the student's skipping class.

As for **(D)**, all you know is that the professor will be angry *if* the student shows up for class, but again, you do not know the consequences of her not showing up, so it's possible that the professor won't be angry.

**(E)**, meanwhile, commits the fallacy of affirming the consequent: there are plenty of other reasons why the professor might be angry, including the other scenario we were given in which the student falls asleep in class.

## 14. (C)

The author's first statement in the paragraph contains the essence of his argument, that a relationship exists between improvisation and band arrangement (or written music) in American jazz. He notes that New Orleans jazz was improvised, Chicago jazz in the '30s was written down (although one soloist had freedom), and '40s jazz relied on total arrangement. Then with bebop improvisation returned, only to be supplanted by written material again in the '70s and '80s. The author notes that there is a relationship between improvisation and arrangements and provides evidence for this back-and-forth swing of the pendulum. Therefore, a probable conclusion for this argument must be **(C)**, which involves the cyclical movement of improvisation and arrangement that the author has noted.

**(A)** is the opposite of **(C)** and denies the author's evidence.

**(B)**, with the word *unfortunate*, is outside the argument because the author is not commenting on the merits of improvisation versus arrangements.

**(D)** contains the word *inconsistencies*, whereas our author points to a relationship that shifts, not one that contains internal contradictions.

**(E)** is about the relationship between soloist and band, not about the larger issue that concerns the author, the relationship between improvisation and arrangement.

### 15. (A)

You are asked here about what the author would probably predict for the next period of jazz. Because you have determined that his point is about the cyclical nature of jazz, and that the last period of jazz has been characterized by "confining arrangement," you can conclude that you are probably entering a period of improvisation.

**(B)** is the same thing as "complicated but confining arrangements," the same style that is in vogue now. You are asked what the author believes will be the next style, and you have no evidence to support the conclusion that the next style will be the same as the present one.

**(C)** was only one aspect of the arranged music emanating from Chicago in the 1930s. Besides, this style was said to follow a period of total improvisation, not total arrangement.

**(D)** comes out of left field. The author mentions no such phenomenon in his survey of jazz history.

**(E)** is too narrow a prediction for our author, whose point concerned the larger issue of improvisation versus arrangement. You can expect a return to total improvisation but not to this specific kind of totally improvised music.

### 16. (D)

The problem with the argument is simply this: Is a "light tank" a light vehicle? Clearly not; a tank is by definition a big, heavy, armor-plated vehicle, and even the lightest tank is a heavy vehicle. The qualifier "light" is thus a relative term and can't be automatically transferred from one class of objects to another class. A light elephant, for instance, is not a light animal. Which one of the choices makes the same mistake of misapplying a relative qualifier? **(D)** copies the flaw exactly; the objects in Professor Wainright's collection may have been soft rocks (say shale or sandstone), but that doesn't mean they can be described as soft objects. Even a soft rock is a hard object, just as even a light tank is a heavy vehicle.

(**A**) does not use a relative qualifier: red is red. Thus, it is perfectly right in saying that if all the flowers are red roses, then they must all be red flowers.

(**B**) makes a different kind of mistake: All X is Y, and all X is Z; therefore, all Y is Z. Basically, (**B**) says that because the property of being a carnivore happens to coincide with the property of being large in this particular collection of zoo bears, the property of being a carnivore must always be accompanied by the property of being large. There's no parallel to the misuse of a relative term in this one.

(**C**), like (**A**), does not use a relative qualifier. A "two-year warranty" means the same thing when applied to a "kitchen appliance" as it does when applied to an "object" in general. Therefore, its argument is sound.

(**E**) follows suit. If all the paintings in the gallery are oil paintings, then any subset of the paintings in the gallery, such as the portraits in the gallery, must also be oil paintings. "Oil painting" doesn't change its meaning when applied to "portrait" and to "painting."

This question is a variation of "equivocation," one of the subtler logical flaws that show up on the LSAT. Equivocation occurs when a term has two or more different meanings and the evidence uses one meaning while the conclusion uses another. In this case, the word *light* means one thing relative to the word *tank*, but this meaning must be tempered somewhat when used to describe the more inclusive category of *vehicle*. The author fails to adjust the meaning of *light* to the different contexts of the evidence and conclusion, thus accounting for the flaw. Once you're aware that such things appear on the LSAT, you should be able to recognize them.

## 17. (A)

This argument operates by making a specific, value-laden statement and then generalizing from that statement. The subject of the first part of the statement is a specific group, while the subject of the second part is a broader category encompassing the first subject. Because situation comedies (one type of television program) are escapist nonsense, then all of television (the second group) is detrimental to children's education. (**A**) is structurally similar to this. Because music (one type of art) soothes the savage breast, then all the arts are beneficial to society's mental health.

**(B)** argues from the specific to the specific. The subject of both parts of the statement is identical, "my brother."

**(C)** and **(E)** are incorrect because they both argue from the general to the specific rather than from the specific to the general. "Drugs" are a category of which aspirin is an example, and "scavengers" are a category of which rats are an example.

**(D)** does not have the same parallel structure that the stem statement and **(A)** have. The subject of its first part, "terrorism," is not a category contained within the subject of the second part, "people."

### 18. (E)

The evidence given in this argument is that a correlation exists between being an Olympic swimmer and having very little body fat. The questionable conclusion is that having very little body fat makes you a better swimmer. Therefore, a causal relationship is being assumed here, when the two factors could just as easily be unrelated (meaning correlation, not causation). Or, more likely, the relationship could be the other way around—being an Olympic swimmer probably causes you to lose a lot of body fat.

The source of the argument is the author, and she certainly doesn't base any conclusion on evidence about herself, so **(A)** is no good.

Nothing in this argument implies that the author thinks her argument is absurd, **(B)**; it may in fact be absurd, but she shows no awareness of this, as **(B)** claims.

**(C)** is incorrect because there's nothing intrinsically flawed about the evidence, it just doesn't prove the conclusion.

Finally, the author doesn't assume her conclusion, so **(D)** is out as well.

### 19. (E)

The author argues that the government should do away with the national speed limit, but the only reason she gives for recommending this course of action is that the fuel shortages that were the original impetus for enacting the legislation are no longer in effect. Her reasoning is supported by the principle described in **(E)**: when the original reason for the enactment of a statute has disappeared, the statute too should be abandoned.

**(A)** is tricky, because it looks a little like correct answer **(E)**. However, the original goal of the statute was to conserve fuel, in response to the fuel shortages of the 1970s, and this goal can still be accomplished by the statute—driving slowly will still save fuel. The only change that's taken place is that there is no longer a fuel shortage, so there's no longer such a pressing reason to save fuel.

In the case of **(B)**, it isn't clear that the statute no longer serves a useful purpose. First of all, it may still be useful to conserve fuel even though the shortage is over; secondly, a speed limit may well serve other purposes, such as saving lives.

**(C)** is doubly flawed. First of all, the author speaks of repealing the statute, not modifying it. Moreover, the author never speaks of "national consensus" as a reason for doing anything.

With **(D)**, the author wants to repeal the statute, not just explain the reasons for its enactment.

If you're having trouble deciding on the correct choice, at least narrow down the choices. It's easy to throw out **(C)** and **(D)** here, because they don't say anything about repealing the statute, which is what the author wants to do. When you then focus your attention on a comparison of the more likely choices, it should become obvious that only **(E)** accurately mirrors the situation described in the stimulus.

## 20. (C)

Madeleine thinks that it's unwise for one section of the country to use its political power to enact law that will eventually affect the environment of another section of the country; in fact, she says that this will inevitably happen. Grant denies this—he says that it's unlikely that what happens to the environment in one section will affect another section. So they're committed to disagree over **(C)**.

It's difficult to know what the speakers would say about **(A)**, because they're arguing about the practical effects of causing environmental degradation to occur in another section of the country, not about the moral status of so doing. Moreover, neither speaker says anything about "future generations."

Madeleine never explicitly says that some section of the country has the power described in **(B)**, but her argument is based on at least the theoretical possibility that it might have such power. Grant, too, discusses the wisdom of the practice as if it's possible, without explicitly saying that it is. There's no necessary disagreement here.

You have no idea whether either Grant or Madeleine thinks that the practice they condemn is one that's likely to be pursued, **(D)**. They're arguing for and against such action on a theoretical basis and wouldn't be committed to disagreeing over its actual likelihood.

**(E)** involves a scope shift. Both Madeleine and Grant agree that it's good policy for one section of the country not to destroy the environment of another section, but you have no idea how either one feels about one section of the country attempting to preserve the environment of another.

Don't worry if a stimulus uses terms whose precise meaning may be unclear to you, as with *environmental degradation*. You don't have to relate the term to anything outside the argument, and within the argument, the term's use will always be clear enough.

Look for explicit disagreements on point-at-issue questions; you shouldn't have to figure out whether either speaker is implicitly holding an opinion on the statement. Look for a statement that uses words and concepts explicitly used by both speakers.

# CHAPTER 4: **READING COMPREHENSION**

Reading Comprehension is likely to be the most familiar of the three question types that appear on the LSAT. Most standardized tests have some sort of Reading Comprehension section. However, just because you may be more familiar with passage-based reading questions than logic games doesn't mean you should spend any less time preparing for this section.

Considering the amount of reading required to pursue a career in law, it only makes sense that Reading Comprehension accounts for little over one quarter of your entire LSAT score. This chapter focuses on how best to attack the LSAT reading passages and their questions and better manage your test time so you can be sure to get the highest score possible.

## INTRODUCTION TO READING COMPREHENSION

The LSAT contains one scored Reading Comprehension section, consisting of four passages, each approximately 450 words long and accompanied by 6 to 8 questions, for a total of 26 to 28 questions out of about 101 questions on the test.

LSAT Reading Comprehension passages, much like law school textbooks, are written in dense, scholarly prose and are taken from the following subject areas:

- Social sciences
- Humanities
- Natural sciences
- Law

Despite what many test takers seem to believe, the Reading Comprehension section does not test your ability to read and comprehend the passages so well that you practically memorize what you read. What it does test is your ability to read for the gist of the passage—the author's central, driving point—and how he or she attempts to support it. Doing well on Reading Comprehension involves focusing when you first read the passage on its gist and structure and then knowing how to research the passage later to answer questions about specific details.

Knowing how to approach this section so that you don't get bogged down reading and rereading the passages will help you to score your best on this section. Let's begin by taking a look at a typical LSAT Reading Comprehension passage and question.

# ANATOMY OF A READING COMPREHENSION QUESTION

Following are the LSAT Reading Comprehension directions along with a typical passage and one of the questions that accompany it.

> **Directions:** Each passage in this section is followed by a group of questions to be answered on the basis of what's stated or <u>implied</u> in the <u>passage.</u> For some questions, more than one answer choice could conceivably answer the question. However, your task is to choose the <u>best</u> answer—that is, the response that most completely and accurately answers the question—and to blacken the corresponding oval on your answer sheet.

>     Congress has had numerous opportunities in recent years to reconsider the arrangements under which federal forestlands are owned and managed. New institutional structures merit development because federal forestlands cannot be efficiently managed under the
> (5) hierarchical structure that now exists. The system is too complex to be understood by any single authority. The establishment of each forest as an independent public corporation would simplify the management structure and promote greater efficiency, control, and accountability.

To illustrate how a system for independent public corporations might
(10)   work, consider the National Forest System. Each National Forest would
become an independent public corporation, operating under a federal
charter giving it legal authority to manage land. The charter would
give the corporation the right to establish its own production goals,
land uses, management practices, and financial arrangements within
(15)   the policy constraints set by the Public Corporations Board. To ensure
economic efficiency in making decisions, the Public Corporations Board
would establish a minimum average rate of return to be earned on
assets held by each corporation. Each corporation would be required to
organize a system for reporting revenues, costs, capital investments and
(20)   recovery, profits, and the other standard measures of financial health.
While the financial objective would not necessarily be to maximize profit,
there would be a requirement to earn at least a public utility rate of
return on the resources under the corporation's control.

Such an approach to federal land management would encourage
(25)   greater efficiency in the utilization of land, capital, and labor. This
approach could also promote a more stable workforce. A positive
program of advancement, more flexible job classifications, professional
training, and above all, the ability to counter outside bids with higher
salaries would enable a corporation to retain its best workers. A third
(30)   advantage to this approach is that federal land management would
become less vulnerable to the politics of special interest groups.

As a way of testing this proposal, consideration should be given to
designating a portion of the federal lands, maybe twenty-five percent,
including national forests, for management by public corporations.
(35)   The performance of the corporations would then be compared to the
performance of a comparable federal agency operation. The experiment
would yield valuable information about the comparative performance of
alternative institutional arrangements for managing federal lands and
would provide an element of competition in federal land management
(40)   that does not now exist.

1. The primary purpose of this passage is to

    A. suggest that the National Forest System is plagued by many problems.

    B. argue that it is necessary to restructure the management of federal forestlands.

    C. insist that private corporations be allowed to manage the country's natural resources.

    D. discuss the role of private corporations in the management of the National Forest System.

    E. highlight the competing needs of public agencies managing national resources.

## BREAKING IT DOWN

Here's a breakdown of all the parts of the game and question.

### The Directions

Note that you must answer each question based only on what's *stated* or *implied* in the passage. This is actually good news—no matter how foreign the subject matter may be to you, the answer to any question is right there in the passage. You just have to locate it.

In addition, note that you're looking for the best answer to each question, not the perfect answer. Disregard that business about "one or more of the choices could conceivably be correct"—that's just a bit of legalese thrown in by the test makers to forestall any possible challenges to the test. In fact, each of the four wrong answer choices to a Reading Comprehension question contains something that makes it wrong, while the correct answer tends to be fairly inconspicuous. Thus, using the process of elimination is essential on this question type.

### The Line Numbers

Line numbers are provided for asking questions that refer to specific lines of text in the passage.

### The Passage

LSAT Reading Comprehension passages are written in dense, often academic prose and are adapted from books and journals in the broad areas of (1) the social sciences, (2) the natural sciences, (3) the humanities, and (4) law. Time permitting, you are encouraged to read the passage when you first encounter it, but the focus of this reading should be on the main idea or gist of the passage, not on the mass of supporting details that the passage is bound to contain. Learning to read quickly for the gist of the passage is a skill you can acquire with just a little instruction and practice.

### The Question

In this question, you are asked about the main idea of the passage, which your initial reading of the passage should reveal. There are essentially two types of Reading Comprehension questions: global questions like this one, which ask questions about the passage as a whole, and detail questions, which require you to locate information in the passage to answer very specific questions.

### The Answer Choices

One reason you don't want to spend too much time reading and rereading the passage is that you need to spend sufficient time attacking and eliminating wrong answers. Fortunately, we can teach you ways to recognize and eliminate classic wrong answer choices.

## ATTACKING READING COMPREHENSION STRATEGICALLY

### TIME MANAGEMENT

Time management is a critical issue in the Reading Comprehension section. Most test takers find it impossible to finish all four passages in the 35 minutes allotted. Doing your best on this section requires an aggressive approach to section management. You cannot simply read the passages the way you normally read and then answer the questions in the order they appear on the test. You need to take charge of the situation and develop a strategic approach to this section.

### Step 1: Decide whether to complete the passage or come back to it.

When you first encounter a passage, decide quickly whether to do it now or later. Play to your own strengths. Some passages have six questions, while others have eight, so it's generally best to do the passages with more questions first.

### Step 2: Familiarize yourself with the passage.

Once you've decided to tackle the passage, skim through the questions to get a general sense of what you're up against. Then read enough of the passage to grasp the author's main idea and get a general sense of now the paragraphs are organized.

### Step 3: Attack the questions.

If a question seems hard, go back to it after you've answered the other questions in the set.

### Step 4: Research and prephrase your answers.

As necessary, go back into the passage to locate the answers to specific questions. Where possible, prephrase the answer before you examine the answer choices.

### Step 5: Attack the answer choices.

Choose the answer that comes closest to your prephrase.

Let's take a closer look at how to read the passages.

## ATTACKING THE PASSAGE STRATEGICALLY

The perceived difficulty of a passage's subject matter varies from test taker to test taker. For instance, every LSAT Reading Comprehension section contains one law passage. Some test takers do great on these passages; others find them to be sheer agony. With every practice test you take, take note of the types of passages you tend to do best on. Skip the ugly passages until after you've given the others your best shot. Learn to take the Reading Comprehension section in the order that makes you happy.

How you approach reading the passage may vary according to how difficult you find the subject matter and/or whether you're running into time trouble. Let's look at various strategies for reading the passage depending on time- and/or section-management issues and the difficulty of the passage.

# PLAN A: EARLY PASSAGE/LOTS OF TIME/EASY TO GET THROUGH

If you're not running into time trouble and the passage itself doesn't present serious obstacles, you'll want to read the entire passage. Here are some reading principles that will allow you to do so with maximum efficiency.

### Focus on the Author

LSAT Reading Comprehension tests your understanding of what the author is thinking and doing. The test writers may want you to draw conclusions about why the passage has been written and how it has been put together. Focusing on authorial intent will help you to understand better the passage in general—why it's organized the way it is and the author's purpose in writing it.

### Read the First Third Closely

You should read the first third more closely than the rest of the passage because the passage's topic and scope (the piece of the topic that the author chooses to cover) are revealed here and—quite often—so are the author's main idea and his or her attitude toward the subject. Moreover, the first third almost always hints at the structure that the passage will follow.

### Don't Sweat the Details

Details are in the passage only to illustrate what the author is thinking or doing. Therefore, read details quickly. Trying to comprehend all of the content is a waste of time. Always boil the passage down to its basics.

### Note Paragraph Topics and Make a Roadmap

Paragraphs are the fundamental building blocks of the passage. Therefore, as you read, take note of paragraph topics and make a mental roadmap. Ask yourself: "What's the point of this paragraph? How does it fit into the overall structure of the passage?" You may even want to jot down some short notes about each paragraph as you read through the passage.

### Stop to Sum Up

After you've read through the passage, take a moment to think about how the passage was put together. Sum up the main idea of the passage in your own words.

Here is the passage again if you'd like to practice this strategy.

Congress has had numerous opportunities in recent years to
reconsider the arrangements under which federal forestlands are
owned and managed. New institutional structures merit development
because federal forestlands cannot be efficiently managed under the
(5)   hierarchical structure that now exists. The system is too complex to be
understood by any single authority. The establishment of each forest
as an independent public corporation would simplify the management
structure and promote greater efficiency, control, and accountability.
      To illustrate how a system for independent public corporations might
(10)  work, consider the National Forest System. Each National Forest would
become an independent public corporation, operating under a federal
charter giving it legal authority to manage land. The charter would
give the corporation the right to establish its own production goals,
land uses, management practices, and financial arrangements within
(15)  the policy constraints set by the Public Corporations Board. To ensure
economic efficiency in making decisions, the Public Corporations Board
would establish a minimum average rate of return to be earned on
assets held by each corporation. Each corporation would be required to
organize a system for reporting revenues, costs, capital investments and
(20)  recovery, profits, and the other standard measures of financial health.
While the financial objective would not necessarily be to maximize profit,
there would be a requirement to earn at least a public utility rate of
return on the resources under the corporation's control.
      Such an approach to federal land management would encourage
(25)  greater efficiency in the utilization of land, capital, and labor. This
approach could also promote a more stable workforce. A positive
program of advancement, more flexible job classifications, professional
training, and above all, the ability to counter outside bids with higher
salaries would enable a corporation to retain its best workers. A third
(30)  advantage to this approach is that federal land management would
become less vulnerable to the politics of special interest groups.
      As a way of testing this proposal, consideration should be given to
designating a portion of the federal lands, maybe twenty-five percent,
including national forests, for management by public corporations.
(35)  The performance of the corporations would then be compared to the

performance of a comparable federal agency operation. The experiment
would yield valuable information about the comparative performance of
alternative institutional arrangements for managing federal lands and
would provide an element of competition in federal land management
(40)   that does not now exist.

## PLAN B: NOT MUCH TIME LEFT/HARD PASSAGE

What to do when you encounter a harder passage or when you are running low
on time.

If you're running out of time and/or the passage is difficult to get through, do
the following:

- Read the first third of passage carefully.

- Then read the first sentence of each subsequent paragraph.

- Finally read the last sentence of the passage.

As always, focus on the big picture, not the details. Apply the following reading
principles.

### The Author's Purpose

Ask yourself, "What is the author trying to convey? Why is the passage structured
as it is?"

### The Big Idea

Even in the first third, which you'll be reading carefully, *focus on the big idea(s),* not
the supporting details.

### The Last Sentence

If you're still unsure about the main idea of the passage after reading the first third,
*pay close attention to the last sentence of the passage.* This is where many authors tie
together the loose ends and clarify the main idea of the passage.

Here's another look at our passage, this time with the sections you don't need to read de-emphasized.

Congress has had numerous opportunities in recent years to reconsider the arrangements under which federal forestlands are owned and managed. New institutional structures merit development because federal forestlands cannot be efficiently managed under the
(5)   hierarchical structure that now exists. The system is too complex to be understood by any single authority. The establishment of each forest as an independent public corporation would simplify the management structure and promote greater efficiency, control, and accountability.

To illustrate how a system for independent public corporations might
(10)  work, consider the National Forest System. Each National Forest would become an independent public corporation, operating under a federal charter giving it legal authority to manage land. The charter would give the corporation the right to establish its own production goals, land uses, management practices, and financial arrangements within
(15)  the policy constraints set by the Public Corporations Board. To ensure economic efficiency in making decisions, the Public Corporations Board would establish a minimum average rate of return to be earned on assets held by each corporation. Each corporation would be required to organize a system for reporting revenues, costs, capital investments and
(20)  recovery, profits, and the other standard measures of financial health. While the financial objective would not necessarily be to maximize profit, there would be a requirement to earn at least a public utility rate of return on the resources under the corporation's control.

Such an approach to federal land management would encourage
(25)  greater efficiency in the utilization of land, capital, and labor. This approach could also promote a more stable workforce. A positive program of advancement, more flexible job classifications, professional training, and above all, the ability to counter outside bids with higher salaries would enable a corporation to retain its best workers. A third
(30)  advantage to this approach is that federal land management would become less vulnerable to the politics of special interest groups.

As a way of testing this proposal, consideration should be given to designating a portion of the federal lands, maybe twenty-five percent, including national forests, for management by public corporations.
(35)  The performance of the corporations would then be compared to the

performance of a comparable federal agency operation. The experiment
would yield valuable information about the comparative performance of
alternative institutional arrangements for managing federal lands and
would provide an element of competition in federal land management
(40)  that does not now exist.

## PLAN C: DESPERATE FOR TIME/LAST PASSAGE

### Read the First and Last Sentences

If you're absolutely desperate and running into serious time trouble, you may be able
to glean the main idea of the passage just by *reading the first and last sentences of the
passage.* Then look around for easy questions to answer.

Note, however, that this strategy doesn't always work. It is only recommended
in emergency situations. Nonetheless, if you're ever desperate to locate the main
idea of a passage quickly, these two sentences, statistically speaking, are where this
information is most likely to be distilled.

# ATTACKING THE QUESTIONS

Once you've read the passage, you're ready to attack the questions. In this section, we'll
discuss the different Reading Comprehension question types you'll encounter on the
LSAT: global, structure, detail, inference, and EXCEPT questions. First, however, let's
take a look at an important skill needed for success on the Reading Comprehension
section—recognizing unbiased versus extreme language in the answer choices.

## UNBIASED VERSUS EXTREME LANGUAGE

Correct answers to Reading Comprehension questions tend to use qualified, unbiased
language. This is because extreme language will make an otherwise good answer
wrong. Being able to recognize and eliminate answer choices that are too extreme is
a valuable Reading Comprehension skill.

## Practice Exercise

Check off in the appropriate column whether the following statements are unbiased (U)—and, therefore, acceptable language for Reading Comp answer choices—or extreme (E)—and, therefore, unacceptable.

| Sentence # | Sentence | E | U |
|---|---|---|---|
| 1 | Reporters tend to focus on news stories that they believe will improve ratings. | | |
| 2 | It is impossible that one person could have authored all of the plays we currently consider to have been written by Shakespeare. | | |
| 3 | All inquiries into the nature of the psyche are pointless, because we still do not fully understand the workings of the mind. | | |
| 4 | The melting of the Antarctic ice sheets is one of the several potential threats to the stability of the earth's climate. | | |
| 5 | Though Copernicus is generally associated with the discovery of the sun-centered universe, Aristarchus may have conceived of the idea in 200 BCE. | | |

## Explanations

**Sentence 1 is (U) unbiased.** *Tend to* is a cautious phrase with language that indicates a reasonable choice on a critical reading question.

**Sentence 2 is (E) extreme.** The word *impossible* is extreme, as is the idea that there is absolutely no way that Shakespeare wrote the plays attributed to him. If the sentence said there was a debate about who authored the plays, it would be less extreme.

**Sentence 3 is (E) extreme.** This sentence is extreme, because it says that *all* inquiries into the mind are pointless, which seems pretty unrealistic. Just because we don't understand everything about the mind doesn't mean that trying to study it is a waste of time.

**Sentence 4 is (U) unbiased.** This sentence doesn't take too strong a stand in any direction. It says that the melting of Antarctic ice sheets is one of *several potential* threats to the earth. This is a classic unbiased sentence.

**Sentence 5 is (U) unbiased.** This sentence is unbiased as well, as it talks about Aristarchus in a guarded way, saying he *may* have thought of the sun-centered universe before Copernicus. By being careful and tentative in the assertion, the author keeps it unbiased.

## GLOBAL QUESTIONS

About a quarter of the questions you'll encounter in this section will ask about the passage as a whole. These include questions that ask about the *main idea* or *primary purpose* of the passage. Every passage will have at least one or two global questions, so you may want to answer these questions first.

You shouldn't have to go back to the passage to answer these questions. Instead, concentrate your efforts on *attacking* and *eliminating* wrong answer choices. Common wrong answer choices to global questions include those that do the following:

- Misidentify the topic of the passage.

- Contradict the passage.

- Are too narrow (deal with just one portion of the passage).

- Are too broad (go beyond the scope of the passage).

- Are too extreme.

> Congress has had numerous opportunities in recent years to reconsider the arrangements under which federal forestlands are owned and managed. New institutional structures merit development because federal forestlands cannot be efficiently managed under the
> (5) hierarchical structure that now exists. The system is too complex to be understood by any single authority. The establishment of each forest as an independent public corporation would simplify the management structure and promote greater efficiency, control, and accountability.

To illustrate how a system for independent public corporations might
(10) work, consider the National Forest System. Each National Forest would
become an independent public corporation, operating under a federal
charter giving it legal authority to manage land. The charter would
give the corporation the right to establish its own production goals,
land uses, management practices, and financial arrangements within
(15) the policy constraints set by the Public Corporations Board. To ensure
economic efficiency in making decisions, the Public Corporations Board
would establish a minimum average rate of return to be earned on
assets held by each corporation. Each corporation would be required to
organize a system for reporting revenues, costs, capital investments and
(20) recovery, profits, and the other standard measures of financial health.
While the financial objective would not necessarily be to maximize profit,
there would be a requirement to earn at least a public utility rate of
return on the resources under the corporation's control.

Such an approach to federal land management would encourage
(25) greater efficiency in the utilization of land, capital, and labor. This
approach could also promote a more stable workforce. A positive
program of advancement, more flexible job classifications, professional
training, and above all, the ability to counter outside bids with higher
salaries would enable a corporation to retain its best workers. A third
(30) advantage to this approach is that federal land management would
become less vulnerable to the politics of special interest groups.

As a way of testing this proposal, consideration should be given to
designating a portion of the federal lands, maybe twenty-five percent,
including national forests, for management by public corporations.
(35) The performance of the corporations would then be compared to the
performance of a comparable federal agency operation. The experiment
would yield valuable information about the comparative performance of
alternative institutional arrangements for managing federal lands and
would provide an element of competition in federal land management
(40) that does not now exist.

1. The primary purpose of this passage is to

   A. suggest that the National Forest System is plagued by many problems.

   B. argue that it is necessary to restructure the management of federal forestlands.

   C. insist that private corporations be allowed to manage the country's natural resources.

   D. discuss the role of private corporations in the management of the National Forest System.

   E. highlight the competing needs of public agencies managing national resources.

## Explanation

Here, the main idea of the passage is clearly found in the first paragraph: managing forests as public corporations would have several advantages over the present system. The closest paraphrase of this is **(B)**, which mentions restructuring forest management.

**(A)** is too narrow, completely missing the main drift of the passage. The author mentions the problems referred to in **(A)**, but the focus is on the solution, not the problems. **(C)** and **(D)** refer to private corporations—never discussed in the passage. Also, note the wording in **(C)**; *insist* is too extreme a word to describe a reasoned appeal such as this passage. Finally, **(E)** goes beyond the scope of the passage, referring to the competing needs of various agencies managing national resources while the passage discusses only the National Forest System.

Other global questions ask about the structure or organization of the passage. Try to answer the following based upon your initial reading of the passage:

2. Which of the following best describes the organization of the passage?

    A. A proposal is made, and then supporting arguments are set forth.

    B. One claim is evaluated and then rejected in favor of another claim.

    C. A point of view is stated, and then evidence for and against it is evaluated.

    D. A problem is outlined, and then various solutions are discussed.

    E. Opposing opinions are introduced and then debated.

Some test takers find it helpful to jot down a brief note about each paragraph as they read through the passage. This roadmap can help when answering questions such as this one or when trying to locate the answers to detail questions.

For instance, someone making a roadmap might write the following beside each paragraph: paragraph 1: *need better forest mgmt;* paragraph 2: *how pub corps work;* paragraph 3: *advantages;* paragraph 4: *way to test plan.* In any case, the organization could be summarized as follows: a proposed solution, detailed explanation of solution, some advantages, and a plan to evaluate. The closest paraphrase is **(A)**, which mentions "proposal" and "support" for the proposal.

Note also how each of the wrong answers has wording that makes it clearly wrong. The author evaluates a claim or proposal, as in **(B)**, but never "rejects" it for another. **(C)** is out because the author never gives evidence "against" the proposal. Nor does he mention other "solutions" **(D)**, or "opposing opinions" **(E)**.

## DETAIL QUESTIONS

Most Reading Comprehension questions will ask you about specific details in the passage. On detail questions, you will often have to go back into the passage to research the answer. You should be easily able to locate the relevant information to answer a detail question either by the wording in the question, which will lead you to similar wording in the passage, or your roadmap, which will help you to know where to look.

Wrong answer choices to detail questions commonly do one of the following:

- Contradict the passage.

- Use similar wording but distort what's said in the passage.

- Go beyond the scope of the passage, stating things that aren't said.

- Refer to the wrong part of the passage (in other words, they don't answer the question being asked).

- Use extreme wording.

> **STRATEGY TIP**
> The correct answers to detail questions will almost always be *paraphrases* of information contained in the passage.

Let's try a detail question.

Congress has had numerous opportunities in recent years to reconsider the arrangements under which federal forestlands are owned and managed. New institutional structures merit development because federal forestlands cannot be efficiently managed under the
(5) hierarchical structure that now exists. The system is too complex to be understood by any single authority. The establishment of each forest as an independent public corporation would simplify the management structure and promote greater efficiency, control, and accountability.

To illustrate how a system for independent public corporations might
(10) work, consider the National Forest System. Each National Forest would become an independent public corporation, operating under a federal charter giving it legal authority to manage land. The charter would give the corporation the right to establish its own production goals, land uses, management practices, and financial arrangements within
(15) the policy constraints set by the Public Corporations Board. To ensure economic efficiency in making decisions, the Public Corporations Board would establish a minimum average rate of return to be earned on assets held by each corporation. Each corporation would be required to organize a system for reporting revenues, costs, capital investments and
(20) recovery, profits, and the other standard measures of financial health.

While the financial objective would not necessarily be to maximize profit, there would be a requirement to earn at least a public utility rate of return on the resources under the corporation's control.

Such an approach to federal land management would encourage
(25) greater efficiency in the utilization of land, capital, and labor. This approach could also promote a more stable workforce. A positive program of advancement, more flexible job classifications, professional training, and above all, the ability to counter outside bids with higher salaries would enable a corporation to retain its best workers. A third
(30) advantage to this approach is that federal land management would become less vulnerable to the politics of special interest groups.

As a way of testing this proposal, consideration should be given to designating a portion of the federal lands, maybe twenty-five percent, including national forests, for management by public corporations.
(35) The performance of the corporations would then be compared to the performance of a comparable federal agency operation. The experiment would yield valuable information about the comparative performance of alternative institutional arrangements for managing federal lands and would provide an element of competition in federal land management
(40) that does not now exist.

3. According to the passage, the present problems of federal forestlands derive mainly from

   A. overuse by the population.

   B. inefficient organization.

   C. hostility from special interest groups.

   D. the corporate mentality of Congress.

   E. opposition to reform by government employees.

For this question, your prior work creating a roadmap and summing up the main idea should have come in handy. You know the passage is about forestland management and that the first paragraph discusses what has led to the need for reform. The main cause, says paragraph 1, is structural inefficiency. The correct answer, **(B)**, should jump out at you as a paraphrase of the author's main criticism.

Of the wrong answers, **(A)** public overuse, **(D)** the corporate mentality of Congress, and **(E)** opposition to reform by government workers are never mentioned. **(C)** could be stretched to fit the idea of "political vulnerability" found in the last line, but it's too extreme ("hostility"). Even worse, it doesn't answer the question that was asked, which is about the source of present problems, not the problems per se.

Sometimes the test writers are kind enough to tell you exactly where to look in the passage to research the answer. If your question contains a line reference, go ahead and reread the sentence in the passage containing the line reference. Try to formulate your own answer to the question before looking at the answer choices.

> **STRATEGY TIP**
> Sometimes reading just the sentence that contains the line reference will not be sufficient; you may have to read a few lines before and after the reference to get a sense of the context.

Let's take a look.

4. The author's attitude toward the "hierarchical structure" mentioned in line 5 can best be characterized as

   A. resigned.
   B. admiring.
   C. skeptical.
   D. bitter.
   E. ambivalent.

Questions that ask about the author's tone or attitude toward a subject may be either global or detail, as in this case. As a rule, this type of question is a gift. You simply have to figure out whether the author's attitude to the subject at hand is positive or negative and eliminate answers that go the wrong way. Then get rid of answer choices that are too extreme or that are otherwise off.

Paragraph 1 cites "hierarchical structure" as the basic problem. Thus, the answer here must be negative—strongly negative—but in keeping with with the passage's unemotional tone. "Admiring" **(B)** is out, as is "bitter" **(D)**, which sounds too emotional. The other negative answers are "resigned," "skeptical," and "ambivalent." **(A)** is out because the author is not resigned—he's advocating a change. "Ambivalent"

(E) is wrong because it implies mixed feelings, some positive, some negative. The author never expresses any positive feelings toward the current hierarchy. Thus the answer has to be "skeptical" (C), which is both negative and purposeful.

## INFERENCE QUESTIONS

Inference questions, quite common on LSAT Reading Comprehension, may be either global or detail. Any time you are asked to determine what a passage suggests, what the author implies, or what can be inferred from a passage, you are being asked to draw an inference rather than to find what is explicitly stated in the passage.

Don't get carried away by this distinction, however. The LSAT writers don't want you to infer too much when they ask an inference question. While you may occasionally have to combine information from two parts of the passage or make a deduction, you don't want to go overboard in reading between the lines. In fact, the LSAT writers often invite you to overthink by making a detail question look like an inference question—i.e., asking what the passage *suggests* when the answer is, in fact, explicitly stated.

---

**STRATEGY TIP**

The correct answer to an inference question is the one answer that must be true given what's stated in the passage. Consequently, wrong answer choices on inference questions commonly do one of the following:

- Contradict the passage.
- Use extreme language.
- Go beyond the scope of the passage, suggesting things that aren't said.

---

Let's look at a question.

> Congress has had numerous opportunities in recent years to reconsider the arrangements under which federal forestlands are owned and managed. New institutional structures merit development because federal forestlands cannot be efficiently managed under the
> (5) hierarchical structure that now exists. The system is too complex to be understood by any single authority. The establishment of each forest

as an independent public corporation would simplify the management
structure and promote greater efficiency, control, and accountability.

(10) To illustrate how a system for independent public corporations might
work, consider the National Forest System. Each National Forest would
become an independent public corporation, operating under a federal
charter giving it legal authority to manage land. The charter would
give the corporation the right to establish its own production goals,
land uses, management practices, and financial arrangements within

(15) the policy constraints set by the Public Corporations Board. To ensure
economic efficiency in making decisions, the Public Corporations Board
would establish a minimum average rate of return to be earned on
assets held by each corporation. Each corporation would be required to
organize a system for reporting revenues, costs, capital investments and

(20) recovery, profits, and the other standard measures of financial health.
While the financial objective would not necessarily be to maximize profit,
there would be a requirement to earn at least a public utility rate of
return on the resources under the corporation's control.

Such an approach to federal land management would encourage

(25) greater efficiency in the utilization of land, capital, and labor. This
approach could also promote a more stable workforce. A positive
program of advancement, more flexible job classifications, professional
training, and above all, the ability to counter outside bids with higher
salaries would enable a corporation to retain its best workers. A third

(30) advantage to this approach is that federal land management would
become less vulnerable to the politics of special interest groups.

As a way of testing this proposal, consideration should be given to
designating a portion of the federal lands, maybe twenty-five percent,
including national forests, for management by public corporations.

(35) The performance of the corporations would then be compared to the
performance of a comparable federal agency operation. The experiment
would yield valuable information about the comparative performance of
alternative institutional arrangements for managing federal lands and
would provide an element of competition in federal land management

(40) that does not now exist.

5. The author suggests that administrators of federal forestlands have been handicapped by which one of the following?

    A. The public expectation that federal forestlands will remain undeveloped

    B. The failure of environmental experts to investigate the problems of federal forestlands

    C. The inability of the federal government to compete with private corporations for the services of skilled professionals

    D. The unwillingness of Congress to pass laws to protect federal forestlands from private developers

    E. The difficulty of persuading citizens to invest their capital in a government-run endeavor

Admittedly, the answer to this question is somewhat hard to locate because much of the passage talks directly or indirectly about forest management problems. Paragraph 1 mentions complexity, while paragraph 3 discusses inefficiency, personnel problems, and political issues, any of which could be the answer. **(A)**, **(B)**, **(D)**, and **(E)** are never mentioned, but **(C)** corresponds to the personnel issue.

Note also that the correct answer does not require a major reach. The passage states, in reference to the proposed restructuring: "A positive program of advancement, more flexible job classifications, professional training, and above all, the ability to counter outside bids with higher salaries, would enable a corporation to retain its best workers." Hence, it doesn't take much inferring to conclude that present administrators are hampered by the inability of the federal government to compete with private corporations for the services of skilled professionals.

## EXCEPT QUESTIONS

EXCEPT questions are generally among the toughest of all Reading Comprehension questions. This is because EXCEPT questions require you to go through the answer choices and find information in the passage that will corroborate all of the answer choices *except* the credited response.

*In other words, you're looking for the one answer choice that's wrong.* Because these questions are so tricky and easy to misread, the test writers must alert you to them by writing EXCEPT in capital letters. In addition, because it's recommended that you skip around within a question set and do the easy questions first, you may want to save these questions for last.

---

**STRATEGY TIP**

To avoid "misbubbling" on your answer sheet when you skip around within a section, mark the correct answers in your test booklet and then fill in all the answers to each passage at one time before you move on to the next passage.

---

Let's give one a try.

Congress has had numerous opportunities in recent years to reconsider the arrangements under which federal forestlands are owned and managed. New institutional structures merit development because federal forestlands cannot be efficiently managed under the
(5) hierarchical structure that now exists. The system is too complex to be understood by any single authority. The establishment of each forest as an independent public corporation would simplify the management structure and promote greater efficiency, control, and accountability.

To illustrate how a system for independent public corporations might
(10) work, consider the National Forest System. Each National Forest would become an independent public corporation, operating under a federal charter giving it legal authority to manage land. The charter would give the corporation the right to establish its own production goals, land uses, management practices, and financial arrangements within
(15) the policy constraints set by the Public Corporations Board. To ensure economic efficiency in making decisions, the Public Corporations Board would establish a minimum average rate of return to be earned on assets held by each corporation. Each corporation would be required to organize a system for reporting revenues, costs, capital investments and
(20) recovery, profits, and the other standard measures of financial health. While the financial objective would not necessarily be to maximize profit, there would be a requirement to earn at least a public utility rate of return on the resources under the corporation's control.

Such an approach to federal land management would encourage
(25)  greater efficiency in the utilization of land, capital, and labor. This
approach could also promote a more stable workforce. A positive
program of advancement, more flexible job classifications, professional
training, and above all, the ability to counter outside bids with higher
salaries would enable a corporation to retain its best workers. A third
(30)  advantage to this approach is that federal land management would
become less vulnerable to the politics of special interest groups.

As a way of testing this proposal, consideration should be given to
designating a portion of the federal lands, maybe twenty-five percent,
including national forests, for management by public corporations.
(35)  The performance of the corporations would then be compared to the
performance of a comparable federal agency operation. The experiment
would yield valuable information about the comparative performance of
alternative institutional arrangements for managing federal lands and
would provide an element of competition in federal land management
(40)  that does not now exist.

6. According to the passage, all of the following are potential benefits
   of forming public corporations to manage federal forestlands EXCEPT

   A. less turnover of personnel.

   B. more effective management of natural resources.

   C. the ability to offer competitive salaries.

   D. less vulnerability to special interest groups.

   E. expansion of federal forestland boundaries.

Although some EXCEPT questions require hunting through the entire passage for
the answer, this one is not so bad. Once again, your roadmap should have led you to
research the final paragraph for the answer to this question. Paragraph 3 names three
benefits: efficiency, stable personnel, and less vulnerability to politics. You're looking
for something that's not one of these benefits, and **(A)**, **(B)**, **(C)** and **(D)** all paraphrase
these benefits. Only **(E)**, forestland expansion, is never mentioned.

As we've seen, the key to doing well on Reading Comprehension questions lies in
knowing how to read for the gist of the passage, how to research the passage for
answers to specific questions, and how to spot the correct answer or, alternatively,
how to recognize and eliminate wrong answers.

# CONCLUSION

Now that we've discussed how to handle the passages and the questions, it's time to look at how to manage the Reading Comprehension section as a whole. Here are strategies to keep in mind as you work your way through it.

## READING COMPREHENSION SECTION MANAGEMENT STRATEGIES

### Look for Friendly Passages to Do First

You're under no obligation to do the passages in the order they appear in the section. Because all the passages are about the same length, the first passage you do should be either one with subject matter that appeals to you or one with eight questions rather than six. In addition, if the first third of a passage is extraordinarily confusing or simply boring to the point of distraction, move quickly on to happier hunting grounds. The goal is always to save the most difficult stuff for last.

### Pace Yourself

Remember, you have slightly more than eight minutes on average to handle each Reading Comprehension passage and its associated questions. Don't obsess on the clock, but don't let your time be swallowed up reading and rereading some particularly dense part of a passage.

### Don't Be Afraid to Skim Over the Dense Parts of a Passage

You may encounter passages that contain a preponderance of technical details or difficult concepts, only to find that few if any of the questions deal with the part of the passage that's so dense. Remember, the test makers aren't necessarily testing to see who's smart enough to understand that part of the passage; they may want to see who's clever enough to skim past the details and focus on the gist of the passage instead.

### Feel Free to Adjust Your Reading Style to Time Constraints and the Difficulty of the Passage

As discussed earlier in this chapter, feel free to read early passages in their entirety (just don't get mired in details and keep your focus on the main idea of the passage). As you get to the final passages, time constraints will often require you to do more skimming and more judicious choosing of which questions to do and which to guess on. This is all part of what it takes to do well on the LSAT. This is what the LSAT mindset is all about!

### Circle the Questions You Skip

Put a big circle in your test booklet around the number of any question you skip. That way, you know where to go back to when and if you have the time.

### Always Circle the Answers You Choose

Circle the correct answers in your test booklet but don't transfer the answers to your grid right away. Instead, after you complete a passage, fill in all the answers on your answer sheet at one time.

### Allow Yourself Time for a Final Grid Check

Give yourself enough time for a final check of the grid to make sure you've got an oval filled in for every question in the section. Remember, a blank grid earns you nothing, but a guess often will raise your score!

## TIME-MANAGEMENT STRATEGIES

You now know that the key to doing well on LSAT Reading Comprehension questions lies in learning how to manage your time well so that you have enough time to answer the questions correctly. Make sure you practice this strategic approach to attacking critical reading questions:

- **Step 1: Decide whether to complete the passage or come back to it.** When you first encounter a passage, decide quickly whether to do it now or later. Play to your own strengths. Some passages have six questions while others have eight, so it's generally best to do the passages with more questions first.

- **Step 2: Familiarize yourself with the passage.** Once you've decided to tackle the passage, skim through the questions to get a general sense of what you're up against. Then read enough of the passage to grasp the author's main idea and get a general sense of how the paragraphs are organized.

- **Step 3: Attack the questions.** If a question seems hard, go back to it after you've answered the other questions in the set.

- **Step 4: Research and prephrase your answers.** As necessary, go back into the passage to locate the answers to specific questions. Where possible, prephrase the answer before you examine the answer choices.

- **Step 5: Attack the answer choices.** Choose the answer that comes closest to your prephrase.

Also, make sure you know how to recognize and eliminate wrong answer choices to the various Reading Comprehension question types.

Common wrong answer choices to **global questions** include those that

- misidentify the topic of the passage.
- contradict the passage.
- are too narrow (deal with just one portion of the passage).
- are too broad (go beyond the scope of the passage).
- are too extreme.

Common wrong answer choices to **detail questions** include those that

- contradict the passage.
- use similar wording but distort what's said in the passage.
- go beyond the scope of the passage, stating things that aren't said.
- refer to the wrong part of the passage.
- are too extreme.

Common wrong answer choices to **inference questions** include those that

- contradict the passage.
- go beyond the scope of the passage, suggesting things that aren't said.
- are too extreme.

# PRACTICE SET

## WETLANDS PASSAGE AND QUESTIONS 1–6

Read the passage below and then answer the related questions that follow.

The United States has less than half of the 215 million acres of wetlands that existed at the time of European settlement. Wetland conversion began upon the arrival of European immigrants with their traditional antipathy to wetlands and with the will and technology to dry them out. In the mid-
(5) 19th century, the federal government awarded nearly 65 million acres of wetlands to 15 states in a series of Swamp Land Acts. But the most rapid conversion occurred between the mid-1950s and mid-1970s, when an estimated 450,000 acres per year were lost, primarily to agriculture.

This conversion has meant the loss of a wide range of important wetland
(10) functions. Wetlands inhibit downstream flooding, prevent erosion along coasts and rivers, and help remove or assimilate pollutants. They support scores of endangered birds, mammals, amphibians, plants, and fishes. Wetlands provide aesthetic and open space benefits, and some are critical groundwater exchange areas. These and other public benefits have been lost
(15) to agricultural forestry and development enterprises of all kinds, despite the fact that most of the conversion goals might have been obtained with far less wetland loss through regional planning, stronger regulation, and greater public understanding of wetland values.

At best, existing wetland laws and programs only slow the rate of
(20) loss. Despite the growing willingness of government to respond, wetland protection faces significant obstacles. Acquisition as a remedy will always be limited by severe budget constraints. The Emergency Wetlands Resources Act allocates only $40 million per year in federal funds, supplemented by relatively modest state funds, for wetland purchase. Ultimately, the wetlands
(25) that are protected will be a small percentage of the approximately 95 million acres remaining today. Wetland acquisition by private environmental groups and land trusts adds qualitatively important but quantitatively limited protection. Government incentives to induce wetland conservation through private initiatives are limited and poorly funded.

(30)    Some private developers have recognized that business can protect selected wetlands and still profit. Recreational developments in Florida have benefited from wetland and habitat protection that preserves visual amenities. It is doubtful, however, that these business decisions to save wetlands would have occurred without strong government regulation; the marketplace does
(35)  not generally recognize the public benefits of wetlands for flood control, fish and wildlife, and other long-term values.

One possible strategy is to protect each and every wetland in threatened areas according to stringent permit guidelines that do not distinguish by wetland types or values. This present approach may be environmentally
(40)  desirable, but it has not worked. About 300,000 acres of wetlands are lost each year. An alternative strategy is to develop a regional management approach focused on valuable wetlands in selected areas that are under intense pressure. Broad regional wetland evaluations could identify critical wetland systems that meet particular local and national needs and avoid
(45)  abandonment of any wetlands without careful review of the tradeoffs. Cooperating federal, state, and local interests can then anticipate and seek ways to prevent wetland losses and can guide future development in areas where alternative options exist. There is no general federal authority to conduct such planning for wetland system protection. But there are several
(50)  authorities under which a program to anticipate and prevent wetland losses on an area-wide basis can be developed.

1. The author's primary purpose in this passage is to

   A. trace the historical development of wetland conversion in the United States.

   B. explain how a wetland area develops and thrives.

   C. call attention to an environmental problem and evaluate possible solutions.

   D. describe the encroachment of agricultural forestry on America's wetlands.

   E. present a concept of environmental protection based on the experience of European immigrants.

2. According to the author, the attitude of most business investors towards wetlands preservation is one of

   A. enthusiastic support.

   B. opposition.

   C. agonized indecision.

   D. indifference.

   E. reluctant acquiescence.

3. According to the passage, wetlands can provide all of the following environmental benefits EXCEPT

   A. a means of preventing coastal erosion.

   B. a haven for endangered species.

   C. a medium for groundwater exchange.

   D. a source of fossil fuel.

   E. the assimilation of pollutants.

4. Which of the following best describes the author's attitude toward government acquisition of wetlands, acquisition by private environmental groups, and protection by private developers?

   A. All three are limited in their potential for slowing wetland loss.

   B. Acquisition by government and private groups offers some protection for wetlands, while actions by private developers will speed wetland loss.

   C. All three strategies are promising, and more study is needed to determine which is best.

   D. A combination of all three strategies, in conjunction with regional management, can potentially reverse the trend toward wetland conversion.

   E. Governmental policy has worsened the problem of wetland loss by emphasizing government acquisition in preference to private acquisition and protection by developers.

5. The author states which of the following about wetland loss in the United States?

   A. It is justifiable if adequate flood control devices can be constructed.

   B. It can be prevented if the federal government will double its $40 million yearly allocation for wetland purchases.

   C. It can be halted through a regional management approach.

   D. It occurred most rapidly between the mid-1950s and mid-1970s.

   E. The federal government should preserve the nation's remaining 95 million acres of wetlands.

6. The author mentions the Emergency Wetlands Resources Act (lines 22–23) in order to

   A. illustrate the need for legislation to save wetland areas in the United States.

   B. argue that the federal government prevents various state governments from protecting valuable wetland areas.

   C. give an example of the severe financial obstacles limiting federal acquisition of wetland areas.

   D. indicate how widespread is the perception that wetlands are not worth saving.

   E. point out the lack of private initiatives to induce wetland conservation.

## WOMEN PASSAGE AND QUESTIONS 7–14

Read the passage below and then answer the related questions that follow.

> In order to discuss representation of women as a group rather than, simply, as individuals, we must consider whether women as a group have unique politically relevant characteristics, whether they have special interests to which a representative could or should respond. Can we argue that women
> (5) as a group share particular social, economic, or political problems that do not closely match those of other groups or that they share a particular viewpoint on the solution to political problems? If so, we can also argue that women share interests that may be represented.

Framing the working definition of "representable interests" in this fashion
(10)  does not mean that the problems or issues are exclusively those of the specified
interest group, any more than we can make the same argument about other
types of groups more widely accepted as interest groups. The fact that there
is a labor interest group, for example, reflects the existence of other groups
such as the business establishment, consumers, and government, which in a
(15)  larger sense share labor's concerns but often have viewpoints on the nature
of, or solutions to, the problems that conflict with those of labor. Nor does
our working definition of an interest group mean that all of the potential
members of that group are consciously allied or that there is a clear and
obvious answer to any given problem articulated by the entire group that
(20)  differs substantially from answers articulated by others.

Research in various fields of social science provides evidence that women
do have a distinct position and a shared set of problems that characterize a
special interest. Many of these distinctions are located in the institution in
which women and men are probably most often assumed to have common
(25)  interests, the family. Much has been made of the "sharing" or "democratic"
model of the modern family, but whatever democratization has taken place, it
has not come close to erasing the division of labor and, indeed, stratification,
by sex. Time-use studies show that women spend about the same amount
of time on and do the same proportion of housework and child care now as
(30)  women did at the turn of the last century.

Furthermore, law and public policy continue to create and reinforce
differences between women and men in property and contract matters,
economic opportunity, protection from violence, control over fertility and
child care, educational opportunities, and civic rights and obligations. The
(35)  indicators generally used to describe differences in socioeconomic position
also show that the politically relevant situations of women and men are
different. Women in almost all countries have less education than men, and
where they achieve equivalent levels of education, segregation by field and,
therefore, skills and market value remains.

(40)  To say that women are in a different social position from that of men and,
therefore, have interests to be represented is not, however, the same as saying
that women are conscious of these differences, that they define themselves as
having special interests requiring representation, or that men and women as

groups now disagree on policy issues in which women might have a special
(45)  interest. Studies of public opinion on the status and roles of women show
relatively few significant differences between the sexes and do not reveal
women to be consistently more feminist than men.

7.  With which of the following statements about the status of women would the
author be LEAST likely to agree?

    A.  In the modern family, housework and child care are more equitably divided
than in the past.

    B.  As groups, men and women do not necessarily disagree on issues of interest
to women.

    C.  Women have special interests that representatives could respond to.

    D.  Women do not have full control over issues relating to their own fertility.

    E.  There are significant differences between the rights of men and women to
hold property and make contracts.

8.  This passage was most likely taken from

    A   a list of proposals prepared for legislators by a women's rights group.

    B.  the introduction to a history of women's suffrage.

    C.  an article on women's representation in a political science journal.

    D.  a feature article on women's issues appearing in a national newspaper.

    E.  a U.N. report on the state of women's rights throughout the world.

9. Which of the following would the author apparently consider to be a necessary characteristic of a group having "representable interests" (line 9)?

   A. All the potential members of the group are conscious of their shared interests.

   B. The problems of the group are unique to its members.

   C. The group's proposed solutions to their problems differ radically from those proposed by other groups.

   D. Members of the group are not already represented as individuals.

   E. Members of the group tend to have similar opinions about the handling of particular political problems.

10. It can be inferred from the passage that which of the following statements is true of men and women as groups?

    A. Women have more education than men, yet still face segregation in the labor market.

    B. In public opinion polls on women's issues, men's responses do not differ in a consistent way from those of women.

    C. Developments in recent years have given men more control over child care issues.

    D. Women are becoming more aware of their differences with men than in the past.

    E. Men do not wish to recognize the special interests of women.

11. According to the passage, which of the following do women of today have in common with women living in 1900?

    A. They are represented only as individuals and not as a group.

    B. They spend about the same time on housework.

    C. They experience significant discrimination in employment.

    D. The jobs they hold require fewer skills than jobs held by men.

    E. The proportion of women among those designated as representative is lower than among the represented.

12. Of the following, the author is primarily interested in discussing

    A. the political and economic exploitation of women.

    B. the history of women's demands for representation as a group.

    C. recent changes in the status of women in society.

    D. opposing views concerning women's awareness.

    E. the criteria that would justify group representation for women.

13. The author specifically mentions which of the following as a problem confronting women?

    A. The percentage of women serving as political representatives is smaller than the percentage of women in the population.

    B. Women are in a different socioeconomic position from that of men.

    C. Men differ greatly from women in the answers they propose for women's problems.

    D. Women do not qualify as an interest group, because they have not banded together to pursue common goals.

    E. A lack of educational opportunities has inhibited women from voicing their concerns.

14. The author's discussion of interest groups in the second paragraph functions as

    A. evidence in support of the author's method of inquiry.

    B. a concession to arguments by opponents of the author's interpretation.

    C. an admission that the author's argument will ignore important aspects of the problem.

    D. a refinement of the author's working definition of an interest group.

    E. evidence for parallels between women's interest groups and other interest groups.

# ANSWERS AND EXPLANATIONS

## ANSWER KEY

| | | | |
|---|---|---|---|
| 1. C | 5. D | 9. E | 13. B |
| 2. D | 6. C | 10. B | 14. D |
| 3. D | 7. A | 11. B | |
| 4. A | 8. C | 12. E | |

## WETLANDS PASSAGE (QUESTIONS 1–6)

In the opening paragraph, you learn that the United States has lost more than half of its wetlands in a conversion process that's been going on for centuries. In paragraph 2, the author explains the benefits of wetlands. In the final three paragraphs, the author discusses current and possible strategies for saving the wetlands, with an emphasis on cooperative wetlands management on a regional basis. No overall main idea is stated, but the author's overall view of the situation is, at best, one of guarded optimism—something that becomes important in question 4.

### 1. (C)

The author begins by describing wetland loss (the ongoing process of converting wetland areas to agricultural, industrial, and commercial development) and the resulting environmental problems it creates. This corresponds to the first part of **(C)**. The rest of the passage corresponds to the second part of **(C)**: the author discusses possible strategies for preventing further wetland loss, gives poor marks to several of them, and proposes an alternative.

**(A)** is too narrow: it aptly describes the first paragraph but says nothing about the rest of the passage. As for **(B)**, although the author briefly describes (in paragraph 2) the environmental benefits provided by a thriving wetland area, he never explains how a wetland area develops and thrives. **(D)**, like **(A)**, is too narrow: to describe the encroachment of agricultural forestry on wetlands is only to describe one part of the problem—what about commercial development?—and fails to touch on any possible solutions. **(E)** is way off the mark. Not a notion of environmental protection but rather an environmental problem originated with the first European immigrants.

**2. (D)**

At the end of paragraph 4, the author notes that even the few enlightened business decisions to protect certain wetlands would probably not have happened without strong government intervention, because "the marketplace" doesn't really understand "the public benefits of wetlands for flood control, fish and wildlife, and other long-term social values." In other words, according to the author, most business investors simply don't care about wetland preservation; their attitude is one of indifference **(D)**. If **(A)** were correct, we might not have a problem of wetland loss. The author never says that businesspeople actively oppose wetland preservation **(B)**, only that they don't care enough about preservation to try to minimize the environmental impact of wetland conversion. **(C)**, if true, would have businesspeople trying to decide between the desire to make profits and the desire to preserve wetlands. Yet most business developers, according to the author, would sooner sacrifice the public benefits of wetlands for their own profits. Finally, **(E)** implies that businesspeople have grudgingly accepted preservation when they would have preferred development, but the passage suggests that they proceed with conversion and commercial development with little or no thought for environmental problems.

**3. (D)**

This is a straight detail question, so you should use your roadmap to guide your search. Environmental benefits of the wetlands are discussed in the second paragraph. Fossil fuel, **(D)**, is not mentioned as a benefit provided by wetland areas. In fact, fossil fuel is not mentioned anywhere in the passage. **(A)**, **(B)**, **(C)**, and **(E)** all appear in paragraph 2.

**4. (A)**

Government and private acquisitions are mentioned in paragraph 3. The author says the first "will always be limited by severe budget constraints" and will save only "a small percentage" of remaining wetlands. The second offers "quantitatively limited" protection. Protection by private developers, in paragraph 4, is also treated pessimistically—only "some" developers have tried to combine protection and profit, and the marketplace generally does not favor such an approach. The most straightforwardly pessimistic choice, **(A)**, is the one you want. **(B)** makes a distinction among the three strategies that the passage does not support. **(E)** does the same thing, adding in a government policy bias that's also never suggested. **(C)** makes a recommendation—further study—that doesn't appear in the passage. **(D)** sounds okay until the end—the author never suggests that any policy will actually reverse the trend. All these choices are straightforwardly wrong, and your only problem should be with their wordiness. Try not to get bogged down in minutiae; instead, go straight to the key idea, such as "reverse" in **(D)**, that makes each one wrong.

## 5. (D)

**(D)** is almost a verbatim restatement of the final sentence of paragraph 1, where the author says that the most rapid conversion of wetland areas in this country took place between the mid-1950s and the mid-1970s. This should have been rather easy to find because your roadmap tells you that paragraph 1 is about the current state of wetlands in the United States. **(A)** distorts the reference to flood control at the end of paragraph 4. The author never says that wetland loss is justifiable if flood control devices can be constructed; flood control is only one of many benefits provided by wetlands. As for **(B)**, the author says in paragraph 3 that $40 million is the federal government's yearly allocation for wetland purchases but that, at best, this only slows the rate of wetland loss. The author does not speculate how much money it would actually take to prevent wetland loss. **(C)** is tempting, but the author never says the regional management approach can actually halt wetland loss; the last paragraph indicates that this is one way to slow or minimize losses, so **(C)** goes too far. **(E)** is similarly plausible but wrong. The author perhaps would like to see the nation's remaining wetlands preserved but never states this as a policy goal. In fact, the last paragraph, by focusing on "selected areas that are under intense pressure," implies that the author thinks some further losses are unavoidable.

## 6. (C)

Just after mentioning "severe budget constraints" that limit government acquisition, the author states that the Emergency Wetlands Resources Act (EWRA) allocates "only $40 million per year" in federal funding for wetland purchases. Therefore, the EWRA is an example illustrating the preceding generalization, which is rephrased in **(C)**. **(A)** incorrectly focuses on the need for legislation to save American wetland areas. Although the EWRA is undeniably a piece of legislation, it is clearly meant to illustrate the problem of inadequate federal funding, not the lack of helpful environmental legislation per se. **(B)** is way off the mark; the author never accuses the federal government of interfering with state government efforts. **(D)** is similarly misleading. Although paragraph 4 says the marketplace generally fails to recognize the benefits of wetlands, the author never implies that there's a widespread perception that wetlands are not worth saving or that the EWRA would be evidence of it. Besides, if you have to move to paragraph 4 to make your argument for (**D**), you've already lost. The EWRA is mentioned as an example in paragraph 3. Therefore, its reason for appearing in the passage should be explained in 3 as well. (**E**), finally, refers to the end of paragraph 3, where the author discusses private initiatives to induce wetland conservation. The EWRA, however, is a federal initiative to protect wetlands.

## Women Passage (Questions 7–14)

This passage has a very straightforward outline: paragraphs 1–2 present the author's definition of an interest group, paragraphs 3–5 give evidence that women fit this definition, and the last paragraph qualifies the conclusion. Stop a moment to define for yourself the "big idea" in the passage. Clearly, it is that women are an interest group, or have "representable interests," as it is put in paragraph 2. This idea is raised in the first paragraph, repeated in paragraph 3, and reiterated in paragraph 5 (with the qualification that women may not define themselves as such). Most of the questions deal with this "big idea" in one way or another, so keeping it firmly in mind will help you.

### 7. (A)

In the third paragraph, the author states that the current model of the modern family has not erased the division of labor within the family and that the modern woman spends about the same amount of time on household work as her turn-of-the-century counterpart. (**A**) goes against this information and is, therefore, a statement with which the author would disagree. (**B**) is an accurate paraphrase of the last sentence of the passage. (**D**) and (**E**) can easily be inferred from information in paragraph 4. (**C**) deals with the "big idea" in the passage: according to the author, women do have "representable interests," as defined in paragraphs 1–2 and detailed in paragraphs 3–5. Thus, (**C**) is not a statement with which the author would disagree.

### 8. (C)

In questions about the probable source of a passage, the answer choices often specify both a type of publication and a particular subject area (style and content). The first speaks to the tone of the passage, the second to what the passage is telling the reader. This excerpt deals with the issue of women's representation on a theoretical level and is written in a scholarly and controlled manner. This style would seem to best fit an article that would appear in a journal of political science, and "women's representation" restates the main topic, so **(C)** is the correct answer. **(A)** can be ruled out immediately. Nowhere does this passage concern itself with proposing any practical solutions to women's problems. Besides, this passage does not read like a list. **(B)** doesn't work because the author is dealing here with concerns that go beyond women's suffrage and, in fact, doesn't deal with that particular topic at all. **(D)** is not possible because the style and scope of this passage would make its appearance in a newspaper article unlikely. Finally, **(E)** is incorrect because the author's discussion is too theoretical and narrow in scope to be part of such a report.

### 9. (E)

All of the answer choices for this question can be easily checked by referring back to paragraphs 1 and 2, where the author presents and qualifies the criteria needed for a group to have representable interests. The author presents two of these criteria in question form towards the end of paragraph 1, and **(E)**, which accurately rephrases the second half of this query in the form of a statement, is the best answer. **(A)**, **(B)**, and **(C)** make assertions that the author specifically rejects in paragraph 2; aside from this, their emphatic, unqualified tone (*all, unique, radically*) doesn't match the author's carefully qualified manner. Finally, **(D)** refers back to the first sentence, which simply distinguishes between individual and group representation, without implying that group members can't be represented as individuals.

### 10. (B)

The author compares the relative status of men and women in paragraphs 3–5. **(B)** can be inferred from the last sentence: if women are not more feminist than men in polls, then men's answers are not consistently different from women's. The first part of **(A)** directly contradicts information supplied in paragraph 4, so it can be quickly eliminated, even though its second part might be correct. **(C)** makes an inference that is not warranted. The author states in paragraph 4 that there are differences between women and men in control over child care. However, the exact nature of this difference is never stated, and it is referred to as an ongoing problem, not as one that has suddenly developed "in recent years." As for **(D)**, nowhere does the author imply that women as a group are becoming more aware of their differences with men. In fact, statements in the final paragraph make it clear that many women may be unaware of differences or may not regard them as important. **(E)** is incorrect because the author never implies that men as a group willfully ignore the special interests of women.

## 11. (B)

This is a specific detail question. Women today are directly compared to women at the turn of the century in the last sentence of the third paragraph. There we find that housework and child care are involved. **(B)** is the only answer choice that includes one of these topics, and it immediately becomes clear that this is the correct answer. Although it is possible that **(A)**, **(C)**, **(D)**, and **(E)** are correct factually, the author never directly compares modern women with women of the past in light of the issues these choices involve.

## 12. (E)

The author begins by asking, in essence, whether women should or could be represented as a group. She states some basic prerequisites, qualifying these in the second paragraph. The author goes on to enumerate why women indeed could be considered a valid special interest group. The last paragraph offers a qualification about group consciousness, which is inferably relevant to the issue of group representation. From this outline, you can see that **(E)** best states the author's primary interest of defining a set of necessary characteristics and showing how women appropriately fall within this group definition—with a caveat. Although the author does deal with the political and economic differences between men and women **(A)**, they are discussed only in reference to the larger issue of women's representation, and *exploitation* is a value-loaded word that the author probably would not use. This passage is certainly not a history of women's demands for representation as a group **(B)**, especially because one of the points the author makes is that most women don't define themselves as having special group interests. **(C)** can immediately be ruled out by looking at the first two words: the passage deals with ongoing conditions, not with "recent changes." Finally, **(D)** is off base for two reasons. The author does not present opposing views, and the issue of women's awareness of their special interests is taken up only in the second and fifth paragraphs.

### 13. (B)

The first sentence of the last paragraph states that the socioeconomic position of women is different from that of men. Elsewhere in the passage, this socioeconomic position, which the author implies is inferior to that of men, is identified as a source of problems for women, **(B)**. **(A)** may be factually correct, but the author never addresses this issue in the passage. **(C)** and **(D)** are contradicted by information in paragraphs 5 and 2 respectively. **(E)** is a half-truth: the author asserts that educational opportunities for women are inferior but never argues that this has inhibited women from voicing their point of view.

### 14. (D)

In paragraph 1, the author outlines the broad criteria that would determine whether women as a group have representable interests. In paragraph 2, the author excludes certain possible interpretations of these criteria in a way that narrows down or pinpoints exactly what she does mean. **(D)** best describes what is going on: refinement of the definition. The other answer choices can be eliminated by looking at the way they begin. Paragraph 2 does not contain any "evidence" for anything, **(A)** and **(E)**, by any stretch of the imagination, nor does it contain a concession **(B)** or an admission **(C)**.

# CHAPTER 5: **LAW SCHOOL ADMISSIONS**

## WHERE TO APPLY

The question of where you should apply has two parts. What schools should you consider, regardless of your chances, and which of these schools can you actually get into? Let's begin with the first question.

### WHAT SCHOOLS SHOULD YOU CONSIDER?

According to one study, 58 percent of all law students end up living and working within a one-hour drive of where they went to law school. That's nearly six out of every ten students!

There are many reasons for this surprising statistic. Obviously, a lot of people attend the local law school in the town where they have always lived and want to continue living. Also, since employers tend to interview and hire from nearby law schools, many recent grads stay put. Whatever the explanation, a majority of all law students end up spending more than just the required three years in the city or region where they attend law school.

Despite the importance of law school selection, however, it's frightening how lightly many applicants treat the whole process, even students who spend a great deal of time studying for the LSAT or working on their applications. Horror stories abound—of distant relatives convincing someone to attend State University Law School just because they themselves did 40 years ago or of a student who decides not to apply to a school because his girlfriend's cousin heard that the social life was not so hot.

This point cannot be stressed enough. *Choosing a law school is a major decision in your life and should be treated as such.* There are several factors to consider when choosing where to apply, including reputation, location, and cost.

## Reputation

How much does a law school's reputation matter? The short answer is that it matters very much in your first few years out of law school, when you're looking for your first job or two. Most employers evaluating you at this time will have little else to go on and so will tend to place a lot of weight on school reputation. After a few years, when you've established a reputation and a record of your own, the importance of your alma mater's rep will diminish.

The long answer to the question of academic reputation, however, is a little more complex. Each applicant must look at his or her situation and ask several questions:

- **Am I looking to work for a law firm or to do public service work?**
  Law firms tend to put more emphasis on the reputation of the school.

- **Do I want to stay in the area or have more mobility nationwide?**
  Some schools enjoy strong local reputations as well as strong alumni bases, whereas other schools have a nationwide appeal.

- **How competitive do I want my law school experience to be?**
  Although there are exceptions, as a general rule the schools with better reputations tend to be very competitive.

- **Do I want to consider teaching as an option?**
  Virtually all law school professors come from a handful of top-notch law schools. The same also applies for the most prestigious judicial clerkships.

- **To what extent am I willing to go into debt?**
  The schools with the biggest reputations also tend to have the biggest price tags.

Studies rank the top 50 schools, the top 15 schools, or categorize all schools into four or five levels. (Most of these books can be found in the reference section of your local bookstore.) Many law firms rely heavily on such rankings in making their hiring decisions.

But there are other methods to determine a school's reputation. Speak to friends who are lawyers or law students. Lawyers have a habit of noting who their most formidable opponents are and where they went to law school. Look through law school catalogs and see what schools the professors attended. Finally, ask the placement offices how many firms interview on campus each year, and compare the numbers. Their answers can give you a strong indication of what the law-firm community thinks of a school.

## Location

Location is of prime importance because of the distinct possibility that you'll end up spending a significant part of your life near your law school—three years at the very least. Even under the best of conditions, law school will be a difficult period in your life. You owe it to yourself to find a place where you'll be comfortable. Pick cities or areas you already know you like or would like to live. Pay particular attention to climate. Think about rural areas versus urban centers.

Visit as many law schools as possible, your top two or three choices at the very least. You may be surprised at what you find. Spend some time researching location by visiting *when school is in session*, which is when you'll get the most accurate picture. You should also:

- Buy a local newspaper and scan the real estate ads for prices near campus; check out campus housing to determine whether it's livable.

- Check out transportation options at the law school.

- Take the school's tour so you can hear about the area's good points.

- Look at bulletin boards for evidence of activities.

Finally, don't be afraid to wander into the student lounge and just ask several law students what they think. Most are more than willing to provide an honest appraisal, but be sure to get more than one opinion.

## Costs

Among the cost issues to consider are:

- **State Schools**
  State schools tend to have lower tuition for in-state residents.

- **Urban versus Rural Living Costs**
  Schools in large urban areas will almost invariably have higher living costs than those in rural areas (although the larger cities also tend to have more part-time jobs for second- and third-year students, which can offset the extra cost).

- **Special Loan Programs**
  Many schools now offer special loan repayment or loan forgiveness programs for students who take low-paying public service jobs.

- **Special Scholarship**
  Programs: Many law schools offer special scholarship programs that range from small grants to full three-year rides.

The law school application will tell you what the annual tuition was for the previous year. Many applications will even give you an estimate of living expenses. If you want to dig deeper, call the financial aid office and ask them to send you the breakdown of living expenses of the average law student. Also ask them to send information about any loan forgiveness programs and about scholarships offered by the law school.

## Job Placement

With the legal job market shrinking, the proficiency of a law school's placement office is now a major factor to be considered. If interviews with law students can be believed, the competency of placement officers varies widely. Some see their job as simply setting up on-campus interviews and making sure they run smoothly. Others call and write letters on behalf of students and are constantly selling the school to employers. Some schools direct almost all of their efforts into placing students into private law firms. Other schools provide information on an entire range of opportunities. At some schools students are lucky if the placement office even provides them with a list of alumni in cities in which they'd like to live. At other schools the office calls alumni to hunt for leads.

Ask the placement office for the percentage of graduates in the most recent class who had jobs upon graduation. Don't be fooled by statistics that show 98 percent of all graduates employed. Almost all law students are eventually employed, even if they drive taxis. The key is to determine how many are placed in law jobs *before* they leave law school.

Second, stop by the placement office on your visit and look around. Ask to see the placement library and check whether it's well organized and up to date. Note whether it carries materials on public interest or teaching jobs and how large this section is. Also ask whether a newsletter is published to keep alumni informed of any recent job openings.

Again, talk with law students. Most have very strong opinions about the performance of their placement office. Most students recognize and appreciate when the placement office is making an extra effort.

## Course Selection

One of the nicest things about law schools today is their growing number of course selections and the new areas of law that are opening up. International trade, employment discrimination, sports and entertainment, and environmental law are all areas in which schools are providing more offerings. Many law students nowadays are becoming specialists, because of both personal preference and better marketability. If you're one of the many students who enter law school without a clue about what kind of law they want to practice, look for schools that offer a lot of different areas of study.

Schools list the courses most recently taught in their recruiting brochure, which they will gladly send you. One note of caution: Just because a class has been taught in the past and is listed in the brochure doesn't mean that it's taught every year or will be taught in the future. If you're interested in a particular class, call the registrar's department and find out how often the class has been taught in the past and whether it will be offered again in the future. Ask to speak with the professor who has taught the course in the past.

## Social Life

Although it's an important part of the law school experience, social life should rank near the bottom of the list of factors to consider when choosing a law school. Why? Because your social life at any law school is what you make of it. Almost all law schools have monthly parties or weekly Thursday night get-togethers at local bars. And if you choose to expand that schedule, you can always find a willing accomplice. Furthermore, most schools now have a comparably full range of social organizations.

Examine the area surrounding the law school. During your first year, locale probably won't matter much. But as you get into your second and third years, you'll likely find that you do have some free time, particularly on weekends. Think about whether you want a quiet rural area where canoeing or skiing are readily available or whether you'd prefer a larger city with a vibrant restaurant and nightlife scene.

## Additional Considerations

There are a few other factors that you may want to toss into the equation when deciding which law school is right for you.

**Class Size:** This factor is not as important as it is when choosing a college because, despite what you may read in a catalogue, virtually all first-year classes will be large. Nevertheless, there are some differences between a school such as Georgetown, with more than 2,000 students and a school such as Stanford, with fewer than 800. In the second and third years, the larger schools tend to have more course offerings, whereas the smaller schools focus on smaller class size and more contact between professors and students. Smaller schools also tend to encourage a greater sense of camaraderie and less competition. Larger schools, on the other hand, produce more alumni and thus more contacts when it comes time for your job search.

**Attrition Rates:** Law schools generally try to keep their attrition rate below ten percent. There are exceptions, however, and if the school you're interested in has an attrition rate above ten percent, you should ask an admissions officer why. There may be a reasonable explanation, but you should probably approach the school with some caution.

**Joint-Degree Programs:** are designed to help students pursue two degrees jointly in less time than it would take to earn them separately. Some common examples are the Master of Public Policy (MPP) or the Master of Business Administration (MBA) combined with the law degree. These programs generally take four to five years to complete. Most schools are becoming more daring in this field—indeed, some are now encouraging students to create their own joint-degree program in any area that they choose, as long as it meets both departments' approval. It's not uncommon now to see joint degrees in law and foreign languages, music, or sociology. Check with the schools to see what joint-degree programs are routinely offered, but don't be limited by them. If you have a specialized program in mind, call the registrar's office and see how flexible they are.

**Clinical Programs:** Every law school in the country now offers one or more clinical programs. A clinic is a unique, hands-on opportunity that allows law students to see how the legal system works by handling actual civil cases for people who can't afford an attorney (and getting credit for it at the same time). Not only are these clinics a tremendous learning tool, but they are also the highlight of many law students' three years of study.

Usually the workload is heavy on landlord/tenant disputes or other debt-collection cases. However, many schools are branching out and offering specialized clinics in such areas as child abuse, domestic violence, and immigration. One word of caution: Clinics tend to be popular with students. In many cases, it's very difficult to get a spot in the class, and admission usually depends on the luck of the draw. As a general rule, the schools in large cities have bigger and more clinics because they tend to have more clients.

**Internships:** Like clinical programs, internships are becoming more popular and varied. Internship programs vary widely from school to school, and may include anything from working for an international trade organization in Europe for an entire year to getting three hours credit for part-time work at the local prosecutor's office. Internships are often overlooked by students who are afraid to veer from the traditional path. Yet they can be a welcome break from regular law studies and may also help in the later job search.

**Computer Facilities and Law Library:** Legal research is a big part of your three years in law school. Nothing will frustrate you more than to have a brief due the next day only to find that your library lacks essential volumes on the subject or that the few computers they have are either occupied or not working. If you make a visit to the law schools, check out their facilities. Again, don't be afraid to ask students for their opinions.

## WHERE CAN YOU GET IN?

Let's turn to the second major question in the selection process: "Where do you have a chance of being accepted?"

Anyone who tells you that he can predict where you'll be accepted is fooling himself and, worse, fooling you. Stories of students accepted by a Harvard, Stanford, or Michigan only to be turned down by schools with far less glamorous reputations are common. Yet what is often overlooked is how well the process does work, considering the volume of applications and the amount of discretion exercised by admissions officers.

One reason the admissions process runs smoothly is that all law schools use the combined LSAT score and GPA as the most important determinant in making the decision. This provides a degree of consistency to the admissions process and gives the applicants some direction in deciding where to apply.

## Those Legendary Law School Grids

Each year, LSAC publishes the *Official Guide to ABA-Approved Law Schools* (the LSAT application booklet tells you how to order it). This guide includes a wealth of information on all the accredited law schools in the United States. The schools themselves provide most of the information for the book, including the LSAT scores and GPAs of the most recently admitted class. These are generally presented in grid form and are the single most valuable tool in determining your chances of being accepted at any particular law school.

## Assembling a List of Schools

Most students apply to too few schools. According to LSAC, the average applicant applies to only about five schools. Admittedly, the cost of applications is rising, and sending out ten or more applications can result in an outlay of $500 or more. But keep in mind that if the cost of application presents a real hardship, most schools will waive the application fee—provided you give them a good, credible reason.

Using the grid numbers as a guide for determining your chances of acceptance, you should create a list of schools to apply to, dividing the list into three categories: preferred schools, competitive, and safe schools.

**Preferred Schools:** These are schools you'd love to attend, but your numbers indicate a less than 40 percent chance of admission. Apply to two or three schools in this group. Long shots rarely pay off, but daydreaming about them is always nice.

**Competitive Schools:** Competitive (or "good fit") schools are those where your grid numbers are in the ballpark and where, depending on the rest of your application, you have a decent chance of getting admitted. These are schools where your numbers give you a 40–80 percent chance of admission. These are the schools on which you should focus most of your attention. Applying to four to seven schools in this group is reasonable and increases your odds of getting into at least one school where you are competitive.

**"Safe" Schools:** These schools are not high on your preference list, but your odds of admission are excellent there. Look at the grids and determine two or three schools where your chances of getting in appear to be 80 percent or better. One suggestion for this list would be to pick schools in locations that you particularly like.

# WHEN TO APPLY

Schools send out application forms in August and September, begin accepting applications in October, and start sending out acceptance letters by November. (As proof that they have a heart, most law schools will not begin sending out rejection letters until after the holiday season.) Application deadlines may be in February or March, but because the schools have begun filling their classes in the fall, it is not unusual for more than 75 percent of the anticipated acceptance letters to have been sent by the spring deadline date. This is what's known as rolling admissions, which creates the scenario of unaware applicants who proudly deliver their applications on the deadline date only to find that they have put themselves at a distinct disadvantage.

## The Advantages of Early Application

Does applying early really provide you with an advantage? Yes! Here are the major reasons why.

### Rising Index Numbers

The first reason has to do with index numbers. Your index number is based on the combination of your LSAT score and your GPA. At the beginning of the application process, most schools set an automatic admittance index number. Applicants whose index numbers surpass that figure are admitted quickly with only a cursory look at their application to confirm that they are not serial killers. At the beginning of the process, law schools are always afraid that they'll have too few applicants accepting their offers, which would mean less tuition money and almost certainly some complaints from the school's administrative office. Thus, they usually begin the application process by setting the automatic admittance index number on the low side. Then they gradually increase it as the admission season wears on and they discover that their fears are unfounded.

### Fewer Available Places

Because schools have a tendency to be a little more lenient early in the process, they begin reaching their admission goals fairly quickly. By February, the school may well have sent out more than 75 percent or more of all the acceptance letters it plans to send. Yet, at this point, all of the earlier applicants haven't been rejected. Instead many people are left hanging, just in case better applicants don't start coming through the system. This means that if you apply in March, you're now shooting for fewer possible positions, yet you're still competing against a fairly substantial pool of applicants.

### The "Jading" Effect

If they are candid, admissions officers will admit that by the time they get to the two thousandth essay on "Why I want to go to law school," they're burned out, and more than a little jaded. Essays or applications that might have seemed noteworthy in the beginning now strike the reader as routine.

## WHEN TO START

For the most part, a pre-Halloween application is overdoing it. When schools are just gearing up, you run the risk of documents being misplaced. Pre-Thanksgiving is the preferable choice and assures that you'll be among the early entries. Shortly before Christmas is not as desirable, but should still hold you in good stead. After Christmas and the holidays, however, you're on the downside and may well find yourself among the last 30 percent of all applications received. And if you go with a post-Valentine's Day application—well, you'd better have strong numbers.

Remember that this discussion applies to the date on which your application is *complete*, not just the date on which the school receives your application forms. Applications are not considered complete until the LSAT score, LSDAS (Law School Data Assembly Service) reports, transcripts, and all recommendations have been received. Even though other people are sending these pieces, it's your responsibility to see that they arrive at the law school promptly. This does *not* mean calling the law school three times a week to see if they've arrived. It means prodding your recommenders or your college to send in the necessary documentation. Explain to them the importance of early applications.

If you want to have a complete application at the law schools by, say, late November, you can't start planning just a few weeks in advance. Your campaign for admission should begin five or six months before that deadline—i.e., 18 months before your first day as a law student. We've included, at the end of this section, a schedule that you can use to organize your campaign. As you'll see, you should plan to devote plenty of time to your applications the summer before they're due.

# APPLICATION CHECKLIST

The three major parts of your law school application:

1. The application form
2. The personal statement
3. Recommendations

## THE APPLICATION FORM

- ☐ Working photocopies of applications made
- ☐ Information/addresses/other data gathered
- ☐ Addendums (if any) written
- ☐ Information transferred to actual application
- ☐ Application proofread
- ☐ Final check done

## THE PERSONAL STATEMENT

- ☐ Theme finalized
- ☐ Readers selected and notified
- ☐ First draft written
- ☐ Self-evaluation made
- ☐ Second draft written
- ☐ Comments from readers received
- ☐ Final draft written
- ☐ Final statement proofread

## RECOMMENDATIONS

- ☐ Recommendation writers chosen
- ☐ Recommendation writers on board
- ☐ Informational meeting with recommendation writers conducted
- ☐ Reminders to all recommendation writers sent
- ☐ Notice of complete application received